ESSENTIAL CRETE

Original text by Susie Boulton
Revised and updated by Des Hannigan

© AA Media Limited 2008
First published 1999. Revised 2010

ISBN 978-0-7495-6672-2

Published by AA Publishing, a trading name of AA Media Limited, whose registered office is Fanum House, Basing View, Basingstoke, Hampshire RG21 4EA. Registered number 06112600.

Colour separation by AA Digital Department
Printed and bound in Italy by Printer Trento S.r.l.

A04192
Maps in this title produced from mapping © Freytag-Berndt u.Artaria KG, 1231 Vienna-Austria

About this book

Symbols are used to denote the following categories:

✚ map reference to maps on cover

✉ address or location

☎ telephone number

🕐 opening times

✋ admission charge

🍴 restaurant or café on premises or nearby

Ⓜ nearest underground train station

🚌 nearest bus/tram route

🚉 nearest overground train station

⛴ nearest ferry stop

✈ nearest airport

❓ other practical information

ℹ tourist information office

► indicates the page where you will find a fuller description

This book is divided into six sections.

The essence of Crete pages 6–19
Introduction; Features; Food and drink and Short break

Planning pages 20–33
Before you go; Getting there; Getting around; Being there

Best places to see pages 34–55
The unmissable highlights of any visit to Crete

Best things to do pages 56–79
Great places to have lunch; stunning views; places to take the children and more

Exploring pages 80–185
The best places to visit in Crete, organized by area

Maps
All map references are to the maps on the covers. For example, Malia has the reference ✚ 18J – indicating the grid square in which it is to be found

Admission prices
Inexpensive (under €2); Moderate (€2–€4); Expensive (over €4)

Hotel prices
Prices are per room per night:
€ budget (under €80); €€ moderate (€80–€130); €€€ expensive to luxury (over €130)

Restaurant prices
Price for a three-course meal per person without drinks: € budget (under €12); €€ moderate (€12–€20); €€€ expensive (over €20)

Contents

The essence of...

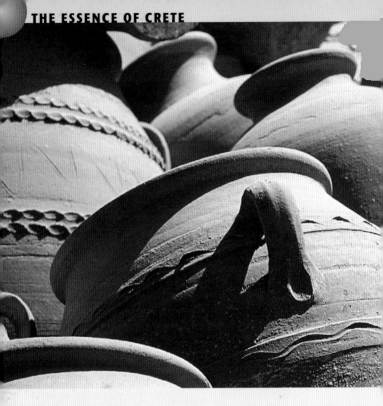

Crete is something of a country in its own right: emphatically Greek, yet with unique traditions of its own. The island's dramatic history is written across the colourful fabric of a landscape that embraces snow-capped mountains, olive groves, timeless villages, cosmopolitan cities and lively beach resorts. It is a landscape signposted by some of the finest ancient sites in the world, symbols of the spectacular Minoan and Mycenaean civilizations. Due to the island's rich agricultural heartland, the local cuisine is delicious, and Crete's religious and folk traditions add excitement to festivals that embrace local and visitor alike with legendary Cretan hospitality.

features

More than any other island in the Mediterranean, Crete has the power to fire the imagination. Ancient ruins and the exquisite works of art they have revealed offer a tantalizing glimpse of Europe's first great civilization: the highly sophisticated Minoans who built the great palace of Knossos, alleged home of King Minos and the Minotaur. The ruins of a Dorian city-state, the mighty ramparts of Venetian fortresses, the soaring minarets of Ottoman mosques, all survive as eloquent evidence of later foreign powers, lured by the island's strategic maritime setting.

Steeped in myth, history and traditions, Crete is also an island of golden beaches and blue seas which has grown to cater to an annual invasion of more than two million visitors. The sands of the north are now skirted by high-rise development, yet in the south small, remote settlements are tucked between spectacular cliffs and the Libyan Sea, some only accessible by ferry or fishing boat. Untouched too is the spectacular mountainous interior of the island where locals go by donkey, Byzantine churches glow with frescoes and rustic villages are lost in time.

Fiercely proud, with a passion for freedom and independence, the islanders regard themselves first as Cretans, secondly as Greeks. Relaxed and friendly, they will readily offer the visitor a glass of *raki*, a slice of raisin bread or a bunch of grapes. It is this warm hospitality,

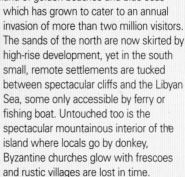

Extra Virgin Olive Oil from Crete

combined with ancient history, natural beauty and sparkling seas, that makes the island, quite simply, unforgettable.

GEOGRAPHY

● Crete is long and thin, extending 250km (155 miles) from east to west and varying from 12km (7.5 miles) to 60km (37 miles) from north to south.
● Crete has 1,046km (649 miles) of coastline.
● Apart from the tiny outpost of Gavdos, Crete is the most southerly of the Greek islands.
● Crete has sunshine on about 300 days a year.

POPULATION

● The population of Crete is 630,000.
● Roughly half the population live in the administrative district of Iraklio, a quarter in Chania and an eighth in both Rethymno and Lasithiou.
● Most of the population live on the north coast.

GOVERNMENT

● Crete is an administrative region of Greece, and sends elected deputies to the Athens parliament.
● The island is divided into four provinces: Chania, Rethymno, Iraklio and Lasithiou.
● Each province has a governor, appointed by the Greek Government in Athens.

TOURISM

● Tourism is overtaking agriculture as the main source of income. Exports of fruit and vegetables are declining as coastal villages turn increasingly to tourism.
● Of the two million tourists that visit Crete annually, the majority are German, followed by Scandinavians and British.

food & drink

Cretan cuisine is based on traditional village cooking and the island is noted for unique food and distinctive local wines. A more adventurous cuisine has developed in recent years, however, and modern Greek dishes, often with an international touch, are sometimes offered.

GREEK FOOD

Establishments serving the traditional Cretan home cooking are worth seeking out – no-frills tavernas, patronized by locals, that are usually found in back streets or rural areas, well away from tourist centres.

Greek menus normally offer a wide choice of starters, followed by meat, fish or vegetable dishes. Frequently, diners are invited into the kitchen to lift the lids and see what's cooking.

Typical starters (*mezedes*), served with a basket of bread, are *taramosalata* (smoked and puréed cod's roe), *tzatsiki* (yoghurt, cucumber and garlic), filo pastry pies, *dolmadhes* (stuffed vine leaves with rice) and such Cretan specialties as *kalitsounia* and *boureki*, delicious savoury pies, or *hohlioi*, snails in a spicy sauce.

Fresh seafood, such as red mullet, swordfish, sea bream, prawns and lobster, can be hard to come by and is often expensive, particularly at harbourside restaurants. Cheaper choices are octopus, squid, whitebait or sardines. In a restaurant the catch of the day will vary according to the time of the year and will normally just be marked 'fresh fish' on the menu with a price per kilo. It's perfectly acceptable to ask the waiter if you can see the fish, and find out what the actual price will be. Seafood such as large succulent prawns, squid, octopus and cuttlefish are likely to be frozen. Although tavernas are obliged to specify on the menu which fish is frozen, many of them don't bother.

The most commonplace meat dish is *souvlaki*, small cubes of pork (or occasionally other types of meat or fish), roasted on a skewer and served with bread, chips and salad. Most menus also feature *moussaka* (minced meat with aubergines and cheese), *stifado* (a meat or fish casserole baked with herbs and tomatoes), and *pastitsio* (macaroni baked with meat). Lamb and chicken, either grilled, roasted or casseroled, are available in

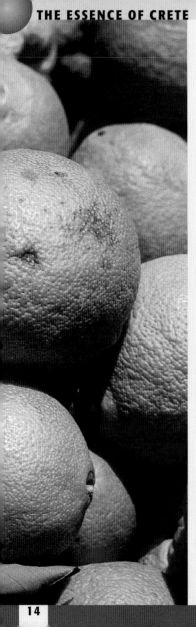

the majority of tavernas. Vegetables are locally grown and particularly delicious. Tomatoes, peppers, aubergines or seasonal vegetables are cooked in olive oil, or often served stuffed with minced meat, rice and herbs. For a change from Greek fare, there are plenty of places serving international dishes, particularly pasta and pizza; there are also a few Chinese restaurants in the main towns.

DESSERTS AND PASTRIES

For dessert locals tend to go to the local pastry shop *(zakharoplasteio)*, which will have a choice of *baklava* (filo pastry with honey and nuts), *kataifa* (shredded pastry with walnuts and syrup) and other sticky treats. Other calorific favourites are *loukoumades* (small round, deep-fried fritters in syrup, served warm), and *bougatsa,* a creamy cheese pastry dusted with icing sugar. Cheese pastries make delicious snacks and are often served with honey as a dessert.

LOCAL RAKI

DRINKING

All restaurants serve Cretan wines; some also have a choice of other Greek varieties and a handful among the more formal restaurants have an international wine list. The dry Cretan bottled red and white wines go well with oily food; the cheap house wine from the barrel, served in tin jugs, traditionally by the kilo, is often surprisingly good. After a meal you may well be offered a complimentary thimble full of raki, perhaps accompanied by a tiny portion of baklava or other sweet pastry.

All bars serve beer – locally brewed Mythos, Amstel and Henninger or imported Heineken and Löwenbräu.

short break

If you only have a short time to visit Crete, or would like to get a rewarding picture of the island, here are the essentials:

● **Learn about Minoan civilization on Crete** by soaking up the atmosphere of the palace of Knossos (➤ 46) or visit Iraklio's Archaeological Museum (➤ 36).

● **Savour a simple meal** of freshly caught fish and a glass or two of Cretan wine, while gazing out over the sea from a family-run taverna with a view.

● **Take a boat trip** around the coast to see otherwise inaccessible beaches and coves, or take a ferry or caïque to an offshore island.

● **Join in the dancing** at a typical Cretan evening in a country taverna – an impromptu event with the locals is best, but even those which have been staged for tourists offer an infectious brand of Cretan fun.

● **Wander around Chania,** one of Crete's most attractive towns, then take some time to relax in a taverna looking out over the picturesque harbour.

● **Take to the streets at festival time** – there are lots of opportunities throughout the year to see colourful processions, fireworks and Cretans having a good time.

● **Go to market** in Iraklio or Chania and be tempted by the enormous range of herbs, spices, raki and honey – the perfect place to make up a picnic.

SPECIAL
CRETAN PRODUCT
HONEY WITH NUTS
CRETE
MICHEL

● **Conjure up images of marauding pirates** at the Venetian fortress in Rethymno, then explore the ancient streets.

● **Head for the hills,** and discover absolute seclusion amid magnificent scenery in one of the rugged mountain ranges – the Lefka Ori (White Mountains), the Ida Mountains or the Dikti massif.

● Hike down the spectacular **Samaria Gorge** – a demanding, but almost compulsory day out (▶ 40).

Planning

DASKALOGIANNIS

Before you go

WHEN TO GO

JAN	FEB	MAR	APR	MAY	JUN	JUL	AUG	SEP	OCT	NOV	DEC
12°C	12°C	14°C	17°C	20°C	24°C	26°C	26°C	24°C	21°C	17°C	14°C
54°F	54°F	57°F	63°F	68°F	75°F	79°F	79°F	75°F	70°F	63°F	57°F

⬤ High season ⬤ Low season

Crete is not quite an all-year destination, as winters can be cold and wet although they will also have their spells of lovely, mild, sunny weather. As Crete is not too far from north Africa it isn't surprising that summers can be very hot, especially in the south of the island.

Crete has a slightly longer and drier season than Greek islands further north, but you can't rule out rain and cold weather at either end of the summer season, in March/April and September/October.

The island is probably at its most beautiful in April/May, when the winter rains ought to have diminished and the spring flowers are in full bloom, especially in the mountains. It is the perfect time for enjoying what Crete has to offer away from the beaches.

WHAT YOU NEED

● Required
○ Suggested
▲ Not required

Some countries require a passport to remain valid for a minimum period (usually at least six months) beyond the date of entry – contact their consulate or embassy or your travel agency for details.

	UK	Germany	USA	Netherlands	Spain
Passport/National Identity Card	●	●	●	●	●
Visa (regulations can change – check before booking your trip)	▲	▲	▲	▲	▲
Onward or Return Ticket	▲	▲	▲	▲	▲
Health Inoculations	○	○	○	○	○
Health Documentation (➤ 23, Health Insurance)	●	●	▲	●	●
Travel Insurance	●	●	●	●	●
Driving Licence (National or International)	●	●	●	●	●
Car Insurance Certificate (if own car)	●	●	●	●	●
Car Registration Document (if own car)	●	●	●	●	●

WEBSITES

The official websites are:
www.visitgreece.gr
www.gnto.co.uk

Visitors may also find the following useful:
www.explorecrete.com
www.crete.tournet.gr

TOURIST OFFICES AT HOME

In the UK

Greek National Tourist Organization (GNTO/EOT)
4 Conduit Street,
London W1S 2DJ
☎ 020 7495 9300

In the USA

GNTO/EOT
Olympic Tower

Suite 903, 645 Fifth Avenue
New York, NY 10022
☎ 212/421-5777

In Canada

GNTO/EOT
1500 Don Mills Road – Suite 102
Toronto, Ontario
M3B 3K4
☎ 416/968-2220

HEALTH INSURANCE

Visitors from the European Union (EU) are entitled to reciprocal state medical care in Greece and should carry a European Health Insurance Card (EHIC). Application forms are available from post offices, or apply online. However, private medical insurance is also recommended, especially for dentistry, which must be paid for up front, as must private medical treatment. You should keep all receipts and then reclaim charges, where applicable, from the Greek authorities.

TIME DIFFERENCES

GMT	Crete	Germany	USA (NY)	Netherlands	Spain
12 noon	2pm	1pm	7am	1pm	1pm

Crete is two hours ahead of Greenwich Mean Time (GMT + 2). The clocks go forward one hour on the last Sunday in March and back one hour on the last Sunday in October.

NATIONAL HOLIDAYS

1 Jan *New Year's Day*	1 May *Labour Day*	26 Dec *St Ste*
6 Jan *Epiphany*	May/Jun *Ascension Day*	
Feb/Mar *'Clean Monday'*	15 Aug *Feast of the*	Restaurants a
25 Mar *Independence Day*	*Assumption*	tourists shops
Mar/Apr *Good Friday* and	28 Oct *Ochi Day*	open on these
Easter Monday	25 Dec *Christmas Day*	museums will

WHAT'S ON WHEN
Festivals

The Greeks have a passion for festivals and fairs, and the Cretans are no exception. Villages celebrate their saint's name day with parades, fireworks, singing and dancing. While some of the island's festivals are strictly religious, others are aimed primarily at tourists. Either way, the celebrations are very colourful events.

January *New Year's Day* (1 Jan): processions, traditional seasonal songs and cutting of the New Year's Cake to find the lucky coin.
Epiphany (6 Jan): blessings of the water; crosses thrown into the sea.

March *Kathari Defteri 'Clean Monday'* (last Monday before Lent): celebrations marking the end of Carnival and beginning of Lent.
Independence Day (25 Mar): military parades.
Holy Week: Greek Orthodox Easter falls up to four weeks either side of the Western festival. This is the most important religious festival in Greece, celebrated with church services, processions, dancing, singing, feasting and fireworks.

May *Labour Day* (1 May): parades and flower festivals.
Commemorations of the Battle of Crete (late May), celebrated in Chania.

July There are festivals and folk performances all over Crete during the busy summer season. Local tourist offices can provide you with information. Iraklio has a summer festival of music, opera, drama, ballet, dancing and jazz.
Cretan Wine Festival (late Jul): a week of wine tasting and dancing in Rethymno.

August *Feast of the Metamorphosis* (6 Aug).
Sultana Festival (mid-Aug): in Sitia.
Feast of the Assumption (15 Aug): Pilgrimage for those named Ioannis (John) to the Church of Agios Ioannis on the Rodopou peninsula, Chania (29 Aug).
Summer in Chania: music, dance, shows.
Renaissance Festival: music, drama and films at the Venetian fortress in Rethymno.

October *Chestnut Festival* (mid-Oct): in Elos and other nearby villages.
Ochi Day ('No' Day, 28 Oct): commemorating the day the Greeks turned down Mussolini's ultimatum in World War II.

November Commemoration in Rethymno and Arkadi of the destruction of the Arkadi monastery in 1866 by the Turks (7–9 Nov).
Feast of the Presentation of the Virgin in the Temple (21 Nov): in Rethymno.

December *Christmas Day* (25 Dec): a feast day, but less significant to the Cretans than Easter.
St Stephen's Day (26 Dec).

Getting there

BY AIR

Iraklio Airport

5 Kilometres to city centre

🚊	N/A
🚌	15 minutes
🚕	10 minutes

Chania Airport

12 Kilometres to city centre

🚊	N/A
🚌	20 minutes
🚕	15 minutes

Sitia Airport

1 Kilometre to city centre

🚊	N/A
🚌	N/A
🚕	10 minutes

Direct charter flights from major European cities, mainly to Iraklio but with some flights to Chania, are available from about Easter to October. EasyJet (www.easyjet.com) has regular flights from London to Iraklio from Easter to early November. There are scheduled flights from Europe and the USA to Athens, from where Aegean Airlines (www.aegeanairlines.gr) and Olympic Air (www.olympicair.com) fly daily to Iraklio and Chania. Sky Express (www.skyexpress.gr) has daily flights from Athens to Iraklio and Olympic Air has regular flights from Athens to Sitia.

Getting around

BY AIR

Within Greece, the domestic carriers, Aegean Airlines, Olympic Air and Sky Express (see above) have year round-flights between Crete and other Greek islands, including Rhodes, Santorini and Mykonos. Some flights to other islands go through Athens, however.

BY FERRY

There are several ferries per day, or overnight, from the Athens port of Piraeus to Iraklio, Chania and Rethymno. Some are much faster than others, so check sailing times first. There are also slightly less frequent sailings to Agios Nikolaos and Sitia. If you want to take your car to Crete, it almost inevitably means going through Athens first and taking a car ferry from there. In summer there are daily fast-ferry connections between Iraklio and Santorini, and conventional ferries between Sitia and Santorini. There are conventional ferries from Iraklio and Sitia to Milos and Rhodes.

PUBLIC TRANSPORT

Buses Crete has an extensive network of buses, providing a cheap and reasonably reliable service throughout the island. There is an excellent service along the main highway linking Agios Nikolaos, Iraklio, Rethymno and Chania. From these towns there are services to smaller towns and most villages. Iraklio has two bus stations, operating services to different regions. The main one, Bus Station A, is near the ferry quays and has services to the main cities and to the east of Crete. Bus Station B is in the west of the city and has services to the west and southwest of the island. Only buses within Iraklio are numbered – others show the destination (not always the right one) on the front of the bus. Local bus timetables are available from bus stations, local tourist offices and sometimes at bus stops. You need to flag down the bus as it approaches.

Timetables are available at main bus stations, or perhaps pinned to a tree or in the café window in more remote villages. Services are operated by the KTEL co-operative. For timetables for the west of Crete see the website www.bus-service-crete-ktel.com (in English) and for the east of the island, www.ktelherlas.gr (Greek only).

Boat trips Boat excursions operate from May to October. Popular trips include cruises to the offshore islands of Spinalonga, Yaidhouronisi (Chrysi) and Dia. From Kolimbari and Chania there are day excursions to the Diktynna Temple, and from several resorts there are boat trips to unspoilt and otherwise inaccessible beaches. Ferries link the south coast resorts of Palaiochora, Sougia, Agia Roumeli, Loutro and Hora Sfakion (Chora Sfakion). From Sougia, Palaiochora and Hora Sfakion ferries operate to the island of Gavdos, south of Crete.

Urban transport Iraklio also has a city bus service. Buses for the airport leave from a stop on the east side of Platia Eleftherias. Buses for Knossos leave from the city bus station adjacent to Bus Station A.

TAXIS

Taxis on Crete are plentiful and can be hailed in the street or picked up at taxi ranks. Check the meter is switched on or, if there is no meter, agree a price in advance. There are some fixed-price journeys.

FARES AND TICKETS

Travelling in Crete is much cheaper than in most European countries. Bus fares are very reasonable. It is sometimes wise to buy a ticket in advance, especially for morning buses. A few concessions are available, mainly for students and schoolchildren.

DRIVING

- The Greeks drive on the right side of the road.
- Speed limit on some sections of national highway: 100kph (62mph) for cars, otherwise 90kph (56mph).
- Speed limit on country roads: 70kph (43mph).
- Speed limit in built-up areas: 50kph (31mph).
- Seat belts must be worn in both front and rear seats. Children under 10 must sit in the rear.
- Drink-driving is heavily penalized. Tolerance is a blood alcohol level of 0.05 per cent of alcohol; above 0.08 per cent is a criminal offence.
- Fuel is readily available in the towns, but it's wise to fill up if you are touring. Super (95 octane), unleaded, super unleaded and diesel are available. Service stations are open Mon–Fri 7am–7pm, Sat 7am–3pm. Some stay open until midnight and open Sun 7am–7pm.
- Members of motoring organizations are entitled to free breakdown service from the Greek motoring organization, ELPA, ☎ 104 in emergencies. Non-members should dial 174 for assistance.

CAR RENTAL

Crete has numerous car rental firms, including all the internationally known names. Check they include tax, collision-damage waivers and unlimited mileage.

Being there

TOURIST OFFICES

- Odos Xanthoudidou 1,
  (opposite Archaeological
  Museum)
  Iraklio
  ☎ (2810) 246298 or 246299

- Iraklio Airport
  ☎ (2810) 397305

- Odos Akti I. Koundourou 20
  (between the lake and the
  harbour)
  Agios Nikolaos, Lasithiou
  ☎ (28410) 22357

- Delfini Building
  Sofokli Venizelou
  (south of Inner Harbour)
  ☎ (28310) 29148

- Inside the town hall
  Odos Khydonias 29, Chania
  ☎ (28210) 36155; www.chania.gr

- Venizelos Street
  Palaiochora, Chania
  ☎ (28230) 41507

- Waterfront, near Platia
  Polytechniou Sitia,
  Lasithiou
  ☎ (28430) 28300

- Palekastro
  Sitia 72300, Lasithiou
  ☎ (28430) 61546;
  www.palaikastro.com

MONEY

The euro (€) is the official currency of Greece. Banknotes are issued in
denominations of 5, 10, 20, 50, 100, 200 and 500 euros; coins in
denominations of 1, 2, 5, 10, 20 and 50 cents, and 1 and 2 euros.

TIPS/GRATUITIES

Yes ✓ No ✗		
Hotels (if service not inc.)	✓	10%
Restaurants (if service not inc.)	✓	10%
Cafés/Bars (if service not inc.)	✓	10%
Taxis	✓	Change
Porters	✓	25c a bag
Tour Guides	✓	Discretionary
Toilets	✓	Discretionary

POSTAL SERVICES

Post offices in the towns and larger villages are identified by yellow signs. In summer mobile offices operate in tourist areas. Post offices usually open 7:30–2:30 Monday to Friday, but in Iraklio and Chania they're open until 8. Stamps can be bought at shops or kiosks selling postcards.

INTERNET ACCESS

Internet is increasingly available in Crete, with many hotels having WiFi or access via a lobby console or internet room. Internet cafés charge €2–€3 per hour and some stay open 24 hours a day.

TELEPHONES

Public telephones take phone cards. These can be the slot-in type, which usually cost €4, but are short-lived. The best option is the scratch-card type, which, for as little as €5, can give up to three hours use. OTE (Greek Telecom) have telephone exchanges in the larger resorts where you can make calls from booths and pay in cash afterwards.

International dialling codes

From Crete dial:
UK 00 44
Germany 00 49
USA & Canada 00 1
Netherlands 00 31
Spain 00 34

Emergency telephone numbers

General emergency/Police 100
Ambulance 166
Fire 199
Road assistance 104 (ELPA) or 174

EMBASSIES AND CONSULATES

UK ☎ (2810) 224012 (Iraklio)
France ☎ (2810) 285618 (Iraklio)
Germany
☎ (2810) 226288 (Iraklio)
☎ (28210) 68876 (Chania)

Netherlands
☎ (2810) 343299 (Iraklio)
USA (Athens Embassy)
☎ (210) 721 2951

HEALTH ADVICE

Sun advice Crete enjoys sunshine for most of the year. At all times a hat, strong-protection sunscreen and plenty of non-alcoholic fluids are recommended.

Drugs Pharmacies have a large green or red cross outside the shop and sell most internationally known drugs and medicines over the counter or by prescription. Opening hours are the same as those of shops, with a rota system at weekends.

Safe water Tap water is quite safe. Bottled water is available everywhere at a reasonable cost.

PERSONAL SAFETY

The crime rate in Crete is very low. Unescorted women should not be surprised if they attract the Mediterranean roving eye. While petty crime is minimal, it's wise to take simple precautions:

- Safeguard against attracting the attention of pickpockets.
- Leave valuables and important documents in the hotel or apartment safe.
- Lock car doors and never leave valuables visible inside.
- Police assistance: ☎ 100 from any call box

ELECTRICITY

The power supply is 220 volts AC, 50hz; with sockets taking continental 2-round-pinned plugs. Visitors from the UK should bring an adaptor. Visitors from the USA will need a transformer for appliances using different voltages.

OPENING HOURS

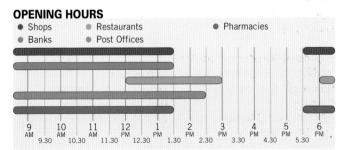

In addition to the times shown above, many shops in tourist areas stay open daily from 8am to late evening. Banks close at the weekend and on public holidays. Opening hours of museums and archaeological sites vary enormously, with many being closed on Mondays.

PLANNING

LANGUAGE

The official language of Crete is Greek. Many of the locals speak English, but a few words of Greek can be useful in rural areas where locals may know no English. It is also useful to know the Greek alphabet – particularly for reading street names and road signs. A few useful words and phrases are listed below, with phonetic transliterations and accents to show emphasis.

yes	*ne*	I don't understand	*katalaveno*
no	*ochi*		*…adio or yasas*
please	*parakalo*	goodbye	*yasoo*
thank you	*efharisto*	sorry	*signomi*
hello	*yasas, yasoo*	how much?	*poso kani?*
good morning	*kali mera*	where is...?	*pou eene..?*
good evening	*kali spera*	help!	*voithia!*
goodnight	*kali nikhta*	my name is...	*meh lene*
excuse me	*me sinchorite*	I don't speak Greek	*then milo hellinika*

hotel	*xenodhohio*	toilet	*twaleta*
room	*dhomatyo*	bath	*banyo*
…single/double	*mono/dhiplo*	shower	*doos*
for three people	*ya tria atoma*	hot water	*zesto nero*
breakfast	*proino*	key	*klidhi*
guest house	*pansyon*	towel	*petseta*

bank	*trapeza*	exchange rate	*isotimia*
exchange office	*ghrafio*	credit card	*pistotiki karta*
	sinalaghmatos	traveller's cheque	*taxidhyotiki epitayi*
post office	*tahidhromio*	passport	*dhiavatiryn*
money	*lefta*	cheap	*ftinos*
how much?	*poso kani?*	expensive	*akrivos*

restaurant	*estiatorio*	dessert	*epidhorpyo*
café	*kafenio*	waiter	*garsoni*
menu	*menoo*	the bill	*loghariazmos*
lunch	*yevma*	bread	*psomi*
dinner	*dhipno*	water	*nero*

wine	*krasi*	waitress	*servitora*
coffee	*kafes*	tea (black)	*tsai*
fruit	*frooto*		
aeroplane	*aeroplano*	...port/harbour	*limani/*
airport	*aerodhromio*		*isitirio*
bus	*leoforio*	single/return ticket	*aplo/metepistrofis*
...station	*stathmos*	car	*aftokinito*
...stop	*stasi*	taxi	*taxi*
boat	*karavi*	timetable	*dhromoloyo*
		petrol	*venzini*

GREEK ALPHABET

The Greek alphabet cannot be transliterated into other languages in a straightforward way. This can lead to variations in romanized spellings of Greek words and place names. It also leads inevitably to inconsistencies, especially when comparing different guidebooks, leaflets and signs. However, the differences rarely make any name unrecognizable. The language looks complex, but it is worth memorizing the alphabet to help with signs, destinations etc.

Alpha	Αα	*short a, as in hat*	Pi	Ππ	*p sound*
Beta	Ββ	*v sound*	Rho	Ρρ	*r sound*
Gamma	Γγ	*guttural g sound*	Sigma	Σσ	*s sound*
Delta	Δδ	*hard th, as in father*	Tau	Ττ	*t sound*
Epsilon	Εε	*short e*	Ipsilon	Υυ	*ee, or y as in funny*
Zita	Ζζ	*z sound*	Phi	Φφ	*f sound*
Eta	Ηη	*long e, as in feet*	Chi	Χχ	*guttural ch, as in loch*
Theta	Θθ	*soft th, as in think*	Psi	Ψψ	*ps, as in chops*
Iota	Ιι	*short i, as in hit*	Omega	Ωω	*long o, as in bone*
Kappa	Κκ	*k sound*			
Lambda	Λλ	*l sound*			
Mu	Μμ	*m sound*			
Nu	Νν	*n sound*			
Xi	Ξξ	*x or ks sound*			
Omicron	Οο	*short o, as in pot*			

Best places to see

1 Archaiologiko Mouseio, Iraklio

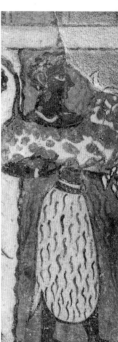

The museum contains the world's richest collection of Minoan art, providing a vivid insight into the life of a highly cultured society.

The rich collection of archaeological finds spans ten centuries, from early neolithic to Roman times; but the main emphasis is on the Minoan era, with treasures from Knossos, Phaistos and other ancient palaces of Crete.

The exhibits range from votive figurines, seal stones, cult vessels and gold jewellery to spearheads and sarcophagi. Outstanding are the exquisite pottery vessels of the Early and New Palace periods, and the tiny figures of animals and people, who are portrayed with an extraordinary degree of naturalistic detail. Among the individual highlights are the Phaistos Disc (➤ 55), the tiny faience figures of the bare-breasted Snake Goddess and her attendant, the bull's head *rhyton,* or ceremonial vessel, and the tiny ivory acrobat in mid-air; and the three carved *rhytons* from Agia Triada (➤ 92): the Chieftain Cup, the Harvester Vase and the Boxer Vase.

The magnificent Minoan frescoes, mostly from the Palace of Knossos (➤ 46), are the highlight of the museum; for although they are heavily restored the lively, vividly coloured

works of art go to the heart of Minoan life from 1600–1400BC.

Those who have visited Knossos may recognize many of the frescoes from the reproductions there, including *The Cup-Bearer* from the Procession fresco, the *Dolphins* from the Queen's apartments, the *Prince of the Lilies* and the famous *Bull-Leapers*. One of the oldest frescoes shows a female figure, nicknamed *La Parisienne*, with an elaborate coiffure, heavy eye make-up and red lips.

✚ *Iraklio 7c* ✉ Platia Eleftherias (entrance on Odos Xanthoudidou), Iraklio ☎ (2810) 224630 ⏰ At the time of writing the museum was undergoing renovation. Meanwhile a temporary exhibition hall displays some of the finest exhibits; Apr–Oct Tue–Sun 8–7:30, Mon 1:30–7:30; Nov–Mar daily 8:30–3 ✋ Expensive; free on Sun in winter 🍴 Cafeteria (€) beside the museum 🚌 Bus stop by the museum ℹ Opposite the museum

2 Cretaquarium

www.cretaquarium.gr

The remarkable Cretaquarium provides an exciting and informative journey for all ages through the Mediterranean's marine wonderland.

Fast becoming one of Crete's top attractions, the Cretaquarium is an integral part of the Hellenic Centre for Marine Research and is one of the largest aquariums in Europe. Educational programmes, functions, lectures and exhibitions underpin its value as a tourist attraction.

The remarkable diversity of the Mediterranean's marine ecosystem is laid out at the aquarium in an informative and entertaining way as the seascape is brought vividly to life in a collection of sixty tanks. The tanks range from huge installations, in which sharks and other large species cruise happily by, to small units containing delicate seahorses and colourful sea anemones. Spiny lobsters, conger eels and Moray eels, groupers and scorpion fish are only a few of the hundreds of Mediterranean and tropical species on display. Touch screen info points, video projectors and other state-of-the-art devices enhance the experience hugely and an easy-to-use audio guide with a choice of nine languages gives in-depth information on how the Mediterranean marine

world functions. Other high points include a tank of beautiful jellyfish that has the impact of a work of art. Special touch pools even allow visitors to handle certain species.

The aquarium has a snack bar, café and restaurant and a colourful gift shop. The building is located on the former American base at Gournies, 14km (9 miles) east of Iraklio, and lies just behind a lovely sandy beach and the glittering Mediterranean itself. Nearby is the **International Exhibition Centre of Crete**, another handsome building that stages major cultural exhibitions.

➕ 17H ✉ Gournies, 14km (9 miles) east of Iraklio
☎ (2810) 337788 🕐 Jun–Sep daily 9–9; Oct–May 9–7
✋ Expensive

International Exhibition Centre of Crete
➕ 17H ✉ Gournies 14km (9 miles) east of Iraklio ☎ (2810)
763300 🕐 Daily 9–9 ✋ Varies depending on exhibition

3 Faragi Samarias (Samaria Gorge)

Towering peaks, plunging depths and springs of clear water – a dramatic setting for a walk through one of Europe's longest and deepest canyons.

In high season up to 2,000 tourists a day walk the 16km (10-mile) gorge. The flood of walkers, mostly on guided tours, kills any real sense of adventure but the stunning mountain scenery is well worth the 5–7 hour hike. The gorge was designated a national park in 1962 in an attempt to preserve its wealth of flora and fauna. Most importantly, the park was created to protect the famous Cretan wild goats, shy, nimble-footed animals that are unlikely to show themselves in the gorge.

The starting point at the head of the gorge is on the mountain-ringed Omalos plain, and by far the best plan is to arrive by public transport, hike through the gorge to Agia Roumeli and take a ferry from here to Hora Sfakion (Chora Sfakion), then a bus back to Chania, the nearest main resort. The walk can be demanding, particularly in the summer

sun: there are mules and a helicopter on hand to help those in trouble. Sturdy walking shoes or boots are essential for negotiating the scree and crossing the river. Those daunted by the prospect of a 16km hike but eager to see the gorge have two options: either to do the first part of the walk, taking the breathtaking descent down the *xiloskala* ('wooden stairs'), with the disadvantage of the stiff climb back; or to start from Agia Roumeli, climbing 2km (1.2 miles) to the entrance, then continuing uphill into the gorge.

✚ 5D ✉ 43km (27 miles) south of Chania ☎ (28210) 67179 or (28210) 67140 🕐 May–Oct, depending on weather, 7–3. From 3pm until sunset visitors are permitted only to walk 2km (1.2 miles) into the gorge, from either end. 👋 Expensive 🍴 Tavernas (€€) at head of gorge and at Agia Roumeli; take refreshments for the gorge 🚌 From Chania to the head of the gorge on the Omalos Plain. From Hora Sfakion back to Chania; check times locally 🚢 In summer 4–5 ferries a day from Agia Roumeli to Hora Sfakion; daily afternoon ferry to Sougia and Palaiochora
❓ For details of walk ➤ 168
ℹ️ Head of the gorge

4 Gortys

The ancient ruins, scattered among fields and hillsides, are eloquent evidence of the power of the former capital of Crete.

Not so ancient as the famous Minoan sites – in fact, rather insignificant in those days – Gortys came to prominence under the Dorians, ousted Phaistos from its pinnacle by the 3rd century BC and attained the ultimate status of capital of Crete after the Roman invasion of 67BC. Its tentacles of power reached as far away as north Africa, but in AD824 the great city was destroyed by the Turks, and it has lain abandoned ever since.

Though the walls have crumbled and the columns have fallen, the extensive remains are a compelling evocation of the great city. The finely preserved apse of the sixth-century Basilica of

Agios Titos is built on the supposed site of martyrdom of St Titus, who was sent by St Paul to convert the islanders to Christianity. Nearby is the semi-circular Odeon, roofless now, but once a covered theatre where the Romans enjoyed

musical concerts. Behind the Odeon, protected now by a modern brick arcade, are perhaps the most precious remains of the site – the huge stone blocks engraved with the famous law code of Gortys which, dating from 500BC, represents the first known code of law in Europe. In its archaic Dorian dialect, written from right to left on one line, then from left to right on the next, the code deals with civil issues such as divorce, adultery, inheritance and property rights, giving a fascinating insight into Dorian life on Crete.

The remnants of the acropolis lie on a hill to the west, and there are more remains along the road towards Agia Deka (but no parking there).

🚹 14K 🖂 Agia Deka, Iraklio (46km/28.5 miles south of Iraklio, 8km/5 miles east of Moires) ☎ (28920) 31144 🕐 Daily 8–6 🖐 Moderate 🍴 Café/bar (€) 🚌 Regular service from Iraklio

5 Chania Limani

One of the most beautiful places on Crete is the Venetian harbour in Chania (also known as Hania).

www.chania.gr

At night, when the sun goes down and the lights come on in the cafés and restaurants, the harbour truly comes into its element. Locals come out for their evening stroll up and down, there are children playing and everyone mixes with the crowds of visitors also enjoying their night out.

The Venetians arrived in the early 13th century, and bought the island of Crete for 100 silver marks from Boniface of Montferrat, who had received the island as part of his share of the spoils after taking part in the Fourth Crusade. The Venetians remained for about 400 years, till the island fell to the Turks. In their time here the Turks built many fortresses, with

their most attractive legacy being this harbour in Chania and some of the lovely old mansions in the Old Towns of both Chania and Rethymno. Several of these have been turned into stylish hotels, and here in Chania some of them have rooftops looking out over the harbour.

Walk west around the harbour and you will come to the remains of the Venetian arsenals, where the builders of the Venetian ships were based. On your way you pass the Mosque of the Janissaries, built in 1645, the year that the Turks captured the town. It is the oldest Turkish building on Crete, and is now a distinguished backdrop to the relaxed and peaceful town of today.

✚ *Chania 2a*
🛈 Inside the town hall, Odos Khydonias 29, Chania
☎ (28210) 36155

6 Knossos

The Minoan civilization grew and prospered around Knossos, the largest and most powerful of the palaces in Crete.

Just over a hundred years ago King Minos and Knossos were merely names from the myths of ancient Greece. Then in 1894 British archaeologist Arthur Evans purchased a site that transpired to be the largest and most important palace in Crete and gave credence to the myths. Excavations, which began in 1900, revealed a complex of buildings, surrounded by a town of around 12,000 inhabitants. The elaborate rooms and the wealth of treasures discovered were evidence of a highly developed ancient civilization, but it was the labyrinth layout and the sacred symbols on walls and pillars that suggested Knossos was the seat of the legendary King Minos and home of the Minotaur. Hence Evans gave the name 'Minoan' to the newly discovered culture.

Site Tour

Raised walkways have been erected around most of the site. Visitors enter by the west court, then follow the walkway to the Corridor of the Procession, with a copy of the original fresco of a procession of over 500 figures. Steps lead up to the *piano nobile*, completely reconstructed and displaying reproductions of the palace's most famous frescoes. From here there are good views over the storerooms and *pithoi* (large storage jars). The terrace steps lead down to the Central Court, formerly used for religious rituals and bull-leaping displays. In the northwest corner the throne room contains the original 'Throne of Minos' and a lustral basin (sunken bath) for purification. The seat in the antechamber is a reproduction of Minos' throne. On the far side of the central court the grand staircase leads down to what Evans believed to be the royal apartments: The Hall of the Double Axes, the King's Megaron and the most elaborately decorated of all the rooms, the Queen's Megaron. This was decorated with the well-known leaping dolphin fresco, and equipped with a bathroom and a lavatory with drains. The walkway continues round to the north entrance, with its reproduction of the Charging Bull fresco, and the theatre and Royal Road, said to be the oldest paved road in Europe.

✚ 16J ✉ 5km (3 miles) south of Iraklio ☎ (2810) 231940
🕐 Daily 8–7:30 (5pm in winter) 💰 Expensive 🍴 Café on the site (€€), tavernas nearby 🚌 No 2 from Iraklio (Bus Station A) every 10 minutes ❓ Guided tours available in four languages. Shop with books and reproductions of finds

7 Moni Arkadiou

The mass suicide within Moni Arkadiou came to symbolize Cretan heroism and strengthened the Cretan struggle against the Turkish yoke.

The fame of Moni Arkadiou lies not so much in its splendid setting on a plateau in the Ida Mountains, nor in its beautiful baroque façade, but in the historic role it played during the struggle for freedom from Turkish rule in the 19th century. Isolated in the mountains, the monastery became an important centre of Cretan resistance, supporting uprisings against foreign powers.

On 9 November 1866, following a two-day siege, thousands of Turkish troops forced entry through the western gateway. Within the monastery hundreds of resistance fighters were taking refuge with their wives and children. Rather than suffer death at the hands of the Turks, the Cretans blew themselves up, so the story is told, by setting light to the powder magazine. Most of the Cretans within the monastery were killed, but so were hundreds of Turks – the exact number of deaths is unknown. Following the event many prominent figures in Europe rallied to support the Cretan cause, among them Garibaldi and Victor Hugo. Nearly a century later the writer Nikos Kazantzakis retold the historic event in his powerful novel, *Freedom and Death*.

Visitors to the monastery can see the richly carved Venetian façade, dating from 1587, the restored interior of the church, the roofless

powder magazine bearing scars of the explosion, and a small museum of icons, vessels and siege memorabilia. Close to the entrance to the monastery an ossuary containing the skulls of the siege victims is a chilling reminder of the events of 1866.

✚ 9D ✉ 24km (15 miles) southeast of Rethymno ☎ (28310) 83116 🕐 Daily 8–7 💵 Moderate 🍴 Snack bar (€) on the premises, taverna (€) at Amnatos (4km/2.5 miles north) 🚌 Four buses a day from Rethymno

8 Moni Preveli

www.preveli.org

The peaceful setting overlooking the southern sea and the monastery's historic past combine to make Preveli one of Crete's most compelling sights.

When Crete fell to the Turks in the 17th century, the monks of Preveli decided to abandon their original monastery in favour of a more secluded location. Their new monastery, perched above the Libyan Sea, soon became a centre of resistance and grew wealthy on the olive groves, sheep, goats, wine,

corn and other gifts that were bequeathed by Cretans to prevent their possessions falling into Turkish hands.

More recently the monastery sheltered Allied troops after the fall of Crete to the Germans in 1941, and assisted their evacuation from nearby beaches to the Egyptian port of Alexandria.

Largely rebuilt in 1835, then partially destroyed by the Germans in reprisal for the protection of the soldiers, the monastery retains none of its original buildings, but it is still a handsome complex with splendid views.

The finest feature is the Church of Agios Ioannis (St John), a 19th-century reconstruction of the original 17th-century church, which has an elaborate inconostasis with many old icons and a gold cross with diamonds, containing what is said to be a fragment of the True Cross. The story goes that the Germans tried three times to steal the cross but each time they attempted to start their escape aircraft, the engines failed. There is a small museum within the church.

The church and remains of the early monastery, Kato Moni Preveli, can still be seen beside the Megapotomos River, 3km (2 miles) inland.

✚ 8E ✉ 13km (8 miles) east of Plakias ☎ (28320) 31246
🕐 Summer daily 9–7; winter daily 9–3. Museum closes 1–3
♿ Moderate 🍴 Snack bar (€) on premises in summer
🚌 Limited bus service from Rethymno

Panagia Kera

The beautifully restored Byzantine frescoes adorning the walls and domes of this tiny church are remarkable for their realism and drama.

Set amid the olive and cypress trees of the Kritsa plain, this delightful little church dates back to the 13th and 14th centuries, and is a treasure house of religious art. Triangular buttresses supporting the aisles give the church an unusual appearance, but it is the interior, with the most complete series of Byzantine frescoes in Crete, that draws the crowds (arrive as early as possible to avoid the crush).

The only light in the church comes through the narrow apsidal windows and it takes time to

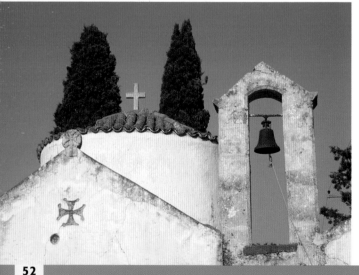

decipher the different scenes. The very oldest frescoes are those of the apse, followed by the scenes from the *Life of Christ* in the dome and nave. More easily recognizable are the nave scenes of *The Nativity*, *Herod's Banquet* and *The Last Supper*.

The later wall paintings of the south and north aisles show a marked move towards naturalism. In the south aisle (where you enter) the scenes from the life of St Anne and of the Virgin Mary are lively 14th-century frescoes, the faces full of expression. Note the face of Anne, whose portrait dominates the apse, and the touching scene in the aisle of Mary looking dejected over Joseph's misunderstood reaction to her conception. An angel descends to explain to Joseph. The north aisle frescoes portray scenes of the *Last Judgement*, depictions of St Anthony and other saints, and a portrait of the founder of the church with his wife and daughter.

➕ 19K ✉ Kritsa, 10km (6 miles) southwest of Agios Nikolaos ☎ (28410) 51711 🕐 Mon–Sat 8:30–2:30, Sun 9–2 🎟 Moderate 🍴 Paradise Restaurant across the road (€€) 🚌 Regular service from Agios Nikolaos ❓ Icons and guides for sale at shop

10 Phaistos

Second only to Knossos in importance, Phaistos dominated the Mesara Plain and was ruled by the legendary Rhadamanthys, brother of King Minos.

The most striking feature of Phaistos is its setting, on a ridge overlooking the Mesara Plain. Excavations by an Italian archaeologist in the early 20th century revealed that the development of Phaistos followed that of Knossos: the palace was built around 1900BC, destroyed in 1700 BC and replaced by a grander palace. Unlike Knossos, however, this second palace (destroyed in 1450BC) incorporated foundations from the first palace. This makes interpretation of the site somewhat confusing and time-consuming and there are no reconstructions (as at Knossos) to help, but the leaflet which comes with the admission ticket is quite useful.

Steps down from the entrance lead to the west court and theatre area via the upper court. The storage structures visible to the south of the west court were probably used for grain.

The grand staircase leads up to the New Palace, with rooms overlooking the Old Palace (fenced off and still undergoing excavation). The huge paved central court, which has fine views of the Psoloreitis range of mountains, was originally bordered by a portico, foundations of which can still be seen.

To the north the royal apartments (currently closed to the public) were the most elaborate of the rooms, with the best views. It was in one of the chambers beyond these apartments, at the northern edge of the site, that the excavators discovered the famous Phaistos Disc, now in Iraklio's Archaeological Museum (➤ 36). Small, round and made of clay, the disc is inscribed with spiralling hieroglyphics that defy translation.

✚ 11F ✉ Phaistos (66km/41 miles southwest of Iraklio, 8km/5 miles west of Moires) ☎ (28920) 42315 🕑 May–Oct daily 8–7:30; Nov–Mar 8–5 ♿ Moderate 🍴 Cafeteria (€) on the premises 🚌 Regular service from Iraklio 🛈 Tourist Pavilion and shop on the premises

Best
things
to do

Great places to have lunch

Akrogiali (€€€)

It is well worth a taxi ride from Chania for this outstanding fish restaurant at the town beach. A delicious speciality is *kakavia*, a fish soup that is more of a filling stew.

✉ Akti Papanikoli 20, Nea Hora, Chania ☎ (28210) 71110 🕓 Mon–Sat 7pm–midnight

Ippokambos (€)

This is one of the liveliest places in town, so get there early or expect to wait. The excellent-value fish dishes and large choice of *mezedes* in this simple taverna near Iraklio's harbour make it popular with locals.

✉ Sofokli Venizelou, Iraklio ☎ (2810) 280240 🕓 Daily

I Trata (€€)

Close to the small town beach of Kitroplatia, the taverna has an inviting rooftop terrace and a menu offering a variety of fish, grilled meat and local Greek fare.

✉ Akti Pagkalou 17, Agios Nikolaos ☎ (28410) 22028 🕓 Daily 11am–midnight

Karnagio (€€)

Tucked away, just round from the main harbour front, this popular eatery offers such treats as a plate of grilled small fish, given added piquancy with Cretan soft cheese and honey.

✉ 8 Platia Katehaki, Old Port, Chania ☎ (28210) 53366 🕓 Apr–Oct daily 10am–midnight

Kastro (€€)

This comfortable taverna has a splendid location with outdoor tables right on the harbourside. Fresh fish and seafood are available most days, and the moussaka is particularly tasty.

✉ Odos Venizelou 169, Sitia ☎ (28430) 23649 🕓 Daily 9am–1am

Limani (€€)

With shaded outdoor tables right beside the beach, this fish taverna makes a good midday break. The Cretan specialities are excellent.

✉ On the Makrygialos waterfront ☎ (28430) 52457
🕐 Daily 10am–noon

Mare (€€)

Escape from Iraklio's tangled main streets to this big waterfront eatery that offers sandwiches and tasty dishes such as wild mushroom or seafood risotto.

✉ Sofokli Venizelou ☎ (2810) 241946; www.mare-cafe.gr 🕐 All day, everyday

Seven Brothers (€€)

The best of several restaurants on Rethymno's inner harbour, serving fresh charcoal-grilled fish.

✉ Rethymno Harbour ☎ (0831) 28956 🕐 All day, every day

Taverna Votomos (€€)

Fresh trout from the nearby hatchery is a speciality at this taverna next to the Idi Hotel, with a pleasant rural setting beside a stream.

✉ Zaros, just outside town ☎ (28940) 31302 🕐 Daily 11am–midnight, weekends only in winter

Vritomartes (€€)

Fresh seafood tops the menu at this popular taverna and you can't beat the location; right in the centre of the harbour area.

✉ Sfiraki waterfront, Elounda ☎ (28410) 41325
🕐 Apr–Oct, daily 10am–11pm

Best beaches

Elafonisi Idyllic pink-tinged sands, in a semi-tropical lagoon. (➤ 164)

Falassarna Huge, beautiful sandy beach, with remarkably few tourists. (➤ 164)

Frangokastello Fine sands and clear waters, suitable for snorkelling. (➤ 166)

Georgioupoli Fine sandy beach stretching several kilometres to the east. (➤ 170)

Matala Beautiful but often crowded south-coast bay, famous for its rock caves. (➤ 98)

Preveli Idyllic creek with a grove of date palms. (➤ 149)

Stavros Scenic bay and beach, with clear shallow waters, on Akrotiri peninsula. (➤ 179)

Sweetwater Beach Long pebble beach known for freshwater springs and nudist campers, reached by boat or foot from Loutro or Hora Sfakion (Chora Sfakion). (➤ 170)

Vai Semi-tropical, otherwise known as Palm Beach. Arrive early to avoid the crowds. (➤ 130)

Yaidhouronisi Uninhabited island, also known as Chrysi, with exotic beaches, reached by excursion boat. (➤ 67)

Top activities

Crete has its own 18-hole golf course, and shorter courses attached to some of the bigger resort-style hotels.

Cycle down a mountain, after being driven to the top. Other organized excursions are widely available.

Get under the clear blue water with one of several diving outfits that cater for beginners in resorts like Malia and Agios Nikolaos.

Hike in the Lefka Ori or in one of the other mountain ranges.

Hike through the spectacular Samaria Gorge (➤ 40), the Impros Gorge (➤ 166) or one of the other scenic gorges in the Chania region.

Hire a car to escape the tourist haunts and explore the peaceful countryside (➤ 132–133).

Horse-riding is available from several stables in different parts of the island, covering everything from sunset beach rides to mountain hacks.

Play tennis at many of the larger resort-style hotels, some of them illuminated to allow tennis to be played into the evenings in summer.

Take a boat trip or ferry to one of the offshore islands or unspoilt coastal villages (➤ 66–67).

Water sports are represented in almost every resort, even small ones, including water-skiing, paragliding, windsurfing and other aquatic thrills.

a walk around Iraklio

Start at Platia Eleftherias (Freedom Square), a traffic-encircled hub of the city.

North of the square visit Iraklio's famous Archaeological Museum (➤ 36–37).

From the inner side of Platia Eleftherias take Odos Dedalou, a narrow pedestrianized shopping thoroughfare leading to Platia Venizelos, the heart of the city.

Try *bougatsa*, a pastry speciality, in one of the cafés overlooking the Morozini Fountain (➤ 91).

With Odos Dedalou on your left, walk to a busy junction. Cross with care and follow the left-hand market street (Odos 1866) to the pretty tree-shaded square of Platia Kornarou.

In the square a café occupies a hexagonal building which was formerly a Turkish water tank; the nearby Venetian Bembo fountain (1588) was assembled using a Roman statue and other antiquities.

Returning along Odos 1866, take the second street on your left, Odos Kosmon, and at the end turn right at Odos 1821 and then left along Odos Moni Odigitrias to reach Platia Agios Ekaterinis.

The square is dominated by the huge neo-Byzantine Cathedral of Agios Minas (1895). In its shadow lies the original, medieval version of Agios Minas, with a splendid iconostatis. On the near side, Agia Ekaterini houses a fine collection of icons (➤ 85; closed for renovations).

With your back to the entrance to Agia Ekaterini go right down Agion Deka. Turn right along Odos Kalokerinou to the junction crossed previously. Turn left past the fountain and continue down Odos 25 Avgoustou.

On the right is Agios Markos (St Mark ➤ 86); further on the arcaded Loggia (today the Town Hall) was the meeting place for Venetian nobility. Just beyond lies Agios Titos (➤ 87).

Continue down the street for the harbour and Venetian fortress (➤ 90).

Distance 3km (2 miles) **Time** 2–5 hours depending on visits
Start Point Platia Eleftherias ✚ *Iraklio 7c*
End Point Harbour ✚ *Iraklio 6a*
Lunch Ippokambos (€) ✉ Odos Sofokli Venizelou ☎ (2810) 280240

Best boat trips

CHANIA

From Chania's Venetian harbour (➤ 44) there are half-day trips in glass-bottom boats, which enable passengers to see the underwater delights too.

DIA

The island of Dia, north of Iraklio (and under the airport's flightpath) can be visited on daytrips from the capital or from Limenas Chersonisou. The Frenchman Jacques Cousteau dived here in search of the lost kingdom of Atlantis and found a Minoan city instead. The day trip includes a barbeque on board the boat with free wine, swimming in clear waters and a chance to see the rare Cretan wild goat *(kri-kri)*.

GAVDOS

Take a ferry from Hora Sfakion (Chora Sfakion, ➤ 170) or Palaiochora (➤ 174) to the island of Gavdos (➤ 167), Europe's most southerly point. This lies 48km (30 miles) offshore, and ferries take about three hours. There are about 40 permanent residents, most of them farmers struggling to earn a living from the parched soil. The landscape is flat and unremarkable, but there are some fine beaches and the turquoise waters are delightful for bathing.

GRAMVOUSA

From Kissamos (➤ 171) in the northwest, a boat leaves daily in summer for the islet of Gramvousa, with its Venetian fortress. The tour goes on to the lagoon of Balos, whose sands and azure waters make for ideal bathing.

RETHYMNO

From Rethymno (➤ 140) there are fishing trips (during the day or at night) and tours to Georgioupoli for fishing, lunch and possible dolphin-spotting. Many of the boats are traditional wooden sailing vessels.

SANTORINI

From some north-coast resorts there are full-day trips to Santorini, one of the Cyclades islands north of Crete. This volcanic island erupted in 1400–1450BC, which may have caused the destruction of the first Minoan palaces on Crete.

Santorini is a strikingly beautiful island of whitewashed houses, volcanic cliffs and beaches of black volcanic sand. The large excursion boats that go there are equipped with bars and restaurants, and during the return journey evening entertainment is provided. The sailing takes three hours each way.

SOUTH COAST VILLAGES

Along the southern coast, ferries are the only link between remote villages such as Loutro and Agia Roumeli, which are inaccessible by road.

SPINALONGA

One of the most popular excursions in the east of Crete is the islet of Spinalonga (➤ 119), north of Agios Nikolaos (➤ 110). There are no beaches here but there is an ancient Venetian stronghold, which played a significant role in Cretan history and was once a leper colony.

YAIDHOURONISI

Off the south coast, a 13km (8-mile) boat trip from Ierapetra (➤ 121), the island of Yaidhouronisi, otherwise known as Chrysi (the Golden Island), has idyllic sandy beaches, clear shallow waters and a small forest of cedar trees.

Stunning views

AMARI VALLEY
This lush valley in south-central Crete (► 150) nestles between high mountains, and great views are all around. One in particular is at a parking and picnic spot, clearly marked south of Agia Foteini.

CHANIA
While Chania is beautiful in its own right, an extra edge is added when you turn a corner and see, framed at the end of the street, the white-capped Lefka Ori mountains of western Crete.

KOUTSOMATADOS RAVINE
On the road south from Kissamos, just before you go through the Tyflos Valley, a dramatic stretch takes you through this ravine, whose walls loom 300m (984ft) above you.

LASITHIOU PLATEAU
High in the Dikti Mountains, the Lasithiou plateau, provides some lovely views, with one of the best being at the pulling-off point by the Taverna Skaranis, just south of the village of Mesa Potamoi.

MOUNT IDA
The highest point on Crete, the 2,456m (8,055ft) top of Mount Ida, provides stunning views whenever you see it, but the best of all are when you drive up towards the summit and the Idaean Cave.

ROUVAS GORGE
Crete is full of scenic gorges, one of the best goes from the little mountain town of Zaros in the Psoloreitis mountains of central Crete. Head up the Rouvas Gorge for a series of impressive views.

SAMARIA
A day hiking down the Samaria Gorge providesone spectacular view after another, although the first time you see one of the breathtaking vistas is the one that will stay with you the most.

Great places to stay

Casa Leone (€€€)

The Casa Leone is a 600-year-old mansion that has been impeccably restored and uses period furnishings. A luxurious getaway with wonderful harbour views.

✉ Odos Parados Theotokopoulou 18, Chania ☎ (28210) 76762; www.casa-leone.com

Elounda Beach Hotel (€€€)

The rooms, bungalows and suites at this exclusive hotel have bay or garden views, marble bathrooms, TVs, bathrobes and fresh flowers. Among the amenities are restaurants, a private beach, heated outdoor pool, health and fitness centre, tennis courts and a water sports centre.

✉ 72 053 Elounda ☎ (28410) 630000; www.eloundabeach.gr

Havania Apartments (€)

With its own swimming pool and little private jetty, this small family-run complex of immaculate apartments is right above the sea, about 2.5km (1.5 miles) from the centre of Agios Nikolaos on the Elounda road.

✉ Agios Nikolaos ☎ (28410) 28758/82458; www.havania.com

Hotel Alianthos Garden (€€)

This informal family-run hotel in Plakias has an outdoor freshwater pool and plenty of activities for children, includng a giant chess set and a playground. There is a choice between hotel rooms and apartments.

✉ Plakias, Rethymno ☎ (28320) 31280; www.alianthos.gr

Milia (€)

Alternative Crete is the style here with 12 rustic stone dwellings, lit by oil lamps (no electricity) and serving organic food.

✉ Milia, Vlatos Kissamou ☎ (28210) 46774; www.milia.gr

Minos Beach Art Hotel (€€€)

Set on a secluded promontory, this top hotel provides luxurious accommodation in the main block or in bungalows.

✉ Agios Nikolaos 72100 ☎ (28410) 22345; www.bluegr.com

Palazzo Rimondi (€€€)

Enjoy luxury suites in several 15th-century Venetian houses that have been converted into the epitome of modern style.

✉ Xanthoudidou 21, Rethymno ☎ (28310) 51289; www.palazzorimondi.com

Palazzo Vecchio (€€)

A genuine restored Venetian 'Palazzo', this boutique hotel is in a quiet area near the sea and just south of the Fortetza. There's a cobbled courtyard and swimming pool. Breakfast is included.

✉ Corner of Iroon Politechniou and Melissinou, Rethymno ☎ (28310) 35351; www.palazzovecchio.gr

Porto Loutro (€)

The only way you can get to this charming hotel, set on Loutro's bay, is by boat or on foot. The best rooms have roof terraces.

✉ Loutro, Hora Sfakion (Chora Sfakion), Chania ☎ (28250) 91433; hotelportoloutro.com 🚤 Regular boat from Agia Roumeli and Hora Sfakion

Places to take the children

IRAKLIO PROVINCE
Aquaplus Water Park
Close to Limenas Chersonisou, Aquaplus offers rides down huge tubes and chutes or more leisurely journeys in rubber rings down the 'Lazy River'. There is also a tropical pool, children's pool and jacuzzi.

✉ Limenas Chersonisou (on the road to Kassamos) ☎ (28970) 24950/1/2/3
🕐 May–Oct daily 10–7 💵 Expensive

Bravo Water and Play Park
Located just to the west of Iraklio, this theme park has swimming pools, water slides, and play areas for youngsters, while parents can relax by the pool.

✉ Ammoudara ☎ (28103) 19334; www.bravopark.gr
🕐 May–mid-Oct daily 10–7 💵 Expensive

Cretaquarium
See pages 38–39.

Minoan Amusement Park
Recreations of ancient palaces make for a fun outing at this theme park 22km (14 miles) west of Iraklio. There's a replica of Ulysses' trireme, a lagoon and a labyrinth.

✉ Agia Pelagia ☎ (28108) 11112; www.capsis.com
🕐 May–Oct daily 10–7 💵 Expensive

Star Beach Water Park
This huge beach and pool complex offers water slides and numerous water-sports facilities, as well as aerobics, mini golf, volleyball and a children's play area. Admission is free and there are separate charges for the individual attractions.

✉ Beach Road, Limenas Chersonisou ☎ (28970) 24472/3; www.starbeach.gr 🕐 Apr–Oct daily 10–7 🚌 Regular service to Iraklio and Malia 💵 Expensive

Water City

This is Crete's most popular water-based leisure park. The complex has huge water slides, chutes, crazy-river rides, a wave pool, water polo and many other water-based activities.

✉ Anopoli, Iraklio ☎ (2810) 781316 🕐 Apr–Sep daily 10–7 🚌 Service from Iraklio and Malia 🖐 Expensive

LASITHIOU PROVINCE
Municipal Beach Club, Agios Nikolaos

The main town beach of Agios Nikolaos has a club with mini golf, children's pool, playground, gardens and snack bar.

✉ Municipal Beach, Agios Nikolaos ☎ None 🕐 Daily 10–6. Closed winter 🖐 Free

RETHYMNO PROVINCE
Rethymno

Boat trips from Rethymno's harbour during summer include Dolphin Cruises, offering a chance to see dolphins along the north coast. There are also daily sailings on two pirate ships.

✉ Venetian Harbour, Rethymno ☎ (28310) 57666 🖐 Moderate

CHANIA PROVINCE
Georgioupoli Boat Trips

The Almiros river flows into the sea at Georgioupoli and you can take paddle boats or canoes along the river to see the turtles (hopefully) and a wide variety of birds.

✉ Georgioupoli Beach 🖐 Inexpensive

Limnoupolis Water Park

This water park is in the west of the island, 8km (5 miles) south of Chania. Facilities include aquatic activities, a restaurant and shops.

✉ Varipetro, Chania ☎ (28210) 33224; www.limnoupolis.gr 🕐 May–Oct daily, all day 🚌 Regular bus service from Chania in season 🖐 Expensive

Best markets

IRAKLIO OPEN-AIR MARKET

A morning stroll along Odos 1866 Monday to Saturday will give you an idea of the wealth of produce from Crete's fertile valleys and hothouses. Bustling, colourful and crowded, the market retains some of the flavour of the bazaar under the Turks and Venetians. Stalls are piled high with peppers, aubergines, beans, zucchini, peaches, cherries, melons and a lot more. Butchers shops are hung with whole carcasses and strings of sausages, leather stalls with bags and belts, small shops with brightly woven rugs and embroidered linen. Grocery shops and stalls are crammed with baskets of spices, jars of wild-herb honey, Cretan mountain tea, olives and nuts, goat and sheep's cheeses. As well as culinary delights there are souvenirs such as sponges and Cretan knives, and everyday goods like wooden spoons, copper coffee pots, knives or hand-made leather boots.

✉ Odos 1866, Iraklio 🕐 Mon, Wed, Sat 8–2, Tue, Thu, Fri 8–2, 5–8:30

IRAKLIO HARBOUR MARKET

A more general street market is held every Saturday morning down around the harbour area. This is much less atmospheric than the open-air market on Odos 1866, with cheap clothes and household goods as well as food, but it gives a glimpse into Iraklio's street life.

✉ Odos Koundourioti, Iraklio 🕐 Sat 8–2

CHANIA MARKET

The splendid market hall was built in 1911, designed on the lines of the marketplace in Marseille. The spectacle of herbs and honeys, oils and spices, dried fruits, cheese, fish, meat, fruit and vegetables is every bit as alluring and lively as the market in Iraklio. This is the

perfect place to buy your picnic. Stallholders will encourage you to taste each variety of cheese and tell you where they are made. A local and distinctive speciality which you can find here is *koulouri* – the dried, elaborately decorated Cretan wedding bread. Insect repellent, applied every three months, preserves the bread.

✉ Platia Sofokli Venizelou, Chania 🕓 Mon, Wed, Thu, Sat 8–2, Tue, Fri 8:30–1:30, 5–8 (summer 6–9)

CHANIA LEATHER MARKET

Close by the covered market hall, Odos Skridlof is the centre for leatherware in Chania. As well as handbags, sandals and other items aimed at the tourist market, you can find some wonderful traditional Cretan mountain boots, mule saddles and other goods made for local consumption.

✉ Odos Skridlof 🕓 Daily 8–10 (less in winter)

RETHYMNO WEEKLY MARKET

A colourful extravaganza of great food and bric-a-brac is staged in Rethymno every Thursday near the public gardens and the old city gate, the Porto Guora. Everything from olives, nails, fruit that tastes like fruit and Cretan herbs, plus clothing, is available.

✉ Odos Dimitrakaki and Odos Koundouriotou 🕓 Thu 8–1

Peaceful towns and villages

AMARI

The main village in the Amari Valley (➤ 150) is a peaceful place
where you can enjoy a coffee or a snack in the taverna in the main
square, as a break from driving through the lovely lush valley.

ARGYROUPOLI

Head into the mountains southwest of Rethymno for this pretty,
quiet village, with its backdrop of the Lefka Ori (White Mountains).

ELOS

Elos is the largest of the nine *kastanochoria*, or chestnut villages,
high in the chestnut forests of western Crete.

KAMPOS

On a winding mountain road about halfway down the west coast
of Crete, villages like Kampos are not over-run with visitors. Here
you will find real Cretan life going on.

NEAPOLI

Only a few kilometres off the northern coast road is the lovely hill
town of Neapoli (➤ 127). They get plenty of visitors here, but it's a
totally different Crete from the one most visitors see.

TOPOLIA

Inland from the busy coastal resorts and roads of northwest Crete
are villages like Topolia, a quiet place of whitewashed houses that
cling to steep mountain slopes: picture-postcard Crete.

VOILA

Crete has several deserted villages in the mountains, and here is
one of the most fascinating. It's in the southeast corner of
Crete, which is a kind of ghost area itself as far as most visitors are
concerned. The roads are often poor, and there are few
large centres.

Great museums and archaeological sites

AGIOS NIKOLAOS ARCHAIOLOGIKO MOUSEIO

While it doesn't compete with the museum in Iraklio (► 36), the Archaeological Museum at Agios Nikolaos is worth visiting as it has some beautiful objects, and the smaller nature of the collection makes it easier to find and appreciate them (► 111).

IRAKLIO ARCHAIOLOGIKO MOUSEIO

The re-opening of the museum, containing the world's richest collection of Minoan art, is eagerly awaited. Meanwhile, you can view some of the finest exhibits in a temporary gallery (► 36).

ISTORIKO MOUSEIO KRITIS

The Historical Museum of Crete (► 88) in Iraklio is an enjoyable museum and should be second on the list for city visitors, after the Archaeological Museum.

KNOSSOS

Anyone remotely interested in the history of Crete must visit the wonderful remains of what was the largest Minoan palace on the island (► 46).

MALIA

Although not as spectacular as Knossos, the archaeological remains of Malia are in a lovely setting (► 96).

MOUSEIO FYSIKIS ISTORIAS KRITIS

Crete's fascinating Natural History Museum is housed in an old power station on Iraklio's western seafront. It is an essential stop to learn about the island's truly wonderful wildlife, past and present (➤ 91).

PHAISTOS

Second only to Knossos in importance, Phaistos is in a wonderfully dramatic setting in southern Crete (➤ 54).

ZAKROS PALACE

The lesser-known archaeological site of Zakros Palace is worth seeing because it does get fewer visitors, and its smaller size gives a more human scale to the buildings and foundations that remain (➤ 130).

Exploring

Crete is the one Greek island that has something for everyone. In part that is because it is the largest Greek island, but it's also because it has always been a proud and independent island, holding onto its traditions.

For most visitors, Crete's superb beaches, especially along the busy north coast with its large resorts, are reason enough to visit. Those interested in history and culture will find satisfaction in the numerous archaeological remains, of which the best-known is the world-famous Knossos, a UNESCO World Heritage Site.

Nature lovers and hikers will discover that Crete is an island filled with secret corners as well as famous places such as the Samaria Gorge. Life in Crete's main cities of Iraklio, Rethymno, Chania and Agios Nikolaos is no less fascinating, with lively crowds, world-class museums, buzzing cafés and top restaurants all adding to the irresistible appeal of this magnificent island.

Iraklio Province

In the centre of the island, Iraklio is the most visited of all the provinces. Not only does it embrace the four great Minoan sites at Knossos, Phaistos, Malia and Agia Triada, but in Limenas Chersonisou and Malia it also has the two biggest resorts on Crete.

Iraklio

Iraklio itself is a bustling, traffic-ridden city but there are increasing areas of pedestrianization and visitors should not miss a visit to the Archaeological Museum, which houses the world's greatest collection of Minoan artefacts. Few tourists stay in the city, most prefer the beach resorts to the east. While the north coast has a long ribbon of tourist development, the south coast is far less accessible, with just a handful of small resorts that range from towns like Matala to villages accessible only by boat or on foot.

IRAKLIO TOWN

Fifth-largest city in Greece, Iraklio is the capital of Crete and the commercial and cultural hub of the island. Herakleium to the Romans, Rabdh-el-Khandak (Castle of the Ditch) to the Saracens, Candia to the Venetians, Megelo Kastro (Great Fortress) to the Turks, it finally reverted to Herakleion (or Iraklio) in 1923. Badly damaged by bombs during World War II, it is today an essentially modern city.

Once a dusty town with an eastern flavour, Iraklio is now taking on a cosmopolitan air. Fashionable young people fill the cafés and smart boutiques sell the latest designs. Everything of cultural interest lies conveniently within the ramparts and can easily be covered on foot. The most colourful quarter is the

harbour, where fishermen gut their catch and skinny cats sniff around for titbits. The fortress overlooking the harbour and the nearby vaults of the arsenals are prominent reminders of the city's Venetian heyday. In the central Platia Venizelos, cafés cluster around the fountain. From here the pedestrianized Odos Dedalou, lined with shops and tavernas, leads on to the huge Platia Eleftherias and the famous Archaeological Museum (➤ 36).

Most of the architecture is postwar, but there are a number of old ruins or fountains, often incorporated into modern buildings, and some neoclassical

buildings. The Venetian walls, 40m thick in places, were constructed in 1462 on earlier Byzantine foundations, and extended in 1538. Most of the gates survive, and you can walk along the line of the walls for about 4km (2.5 miles), though only 1km (0.6 miles) of the walk is actually on top of the walls. Near here is the tomb of Nikos Kazantzakis – Crete's most famous writer.

✚ 16H

Agia Ekaterini (Museum of Religious Art)

Within the Church of Agia Ekaterini (St Catherine), the Museum of Religious Art houses the most important collection of icons in Crete. During the 16th and 17th centuries the church was part of the Mount Sinai Monastery School, which became one of the centres of the 'Cretan Renaissance'. The style of painting was characterized by the intermingling of Byzantine iconography with elements inspired by the Western Renaissance. One of the pupils here was Mikhail Damaskinos, and the six icons by him, on the right as you go in, are the finest works of art in the museum. Domenico Theotokopoulos, commonly known as El Greco, may have been one of his contemporaries.

✚ *Iraklio 5c* ✉ Platia Ekaterinis ☎ (2810) 288825
🕐 Church and museum currently closed for renovation
💰 Moderate 🍴 Cafés (€) in Platia Ekaterinis

Archaiologiko Mouseio

Best places to see ➤ 36–37.

Agios Markos

The Basilica of St Mark, fronted by an arcaded portico, was built in 1239 by the Venetians and dedicated to their patron saint. The first church was destroyed by an earthquake in 1303 and its successor followed the same fate in 1508, but it was rebuilt and, like many others on Crete, became a mosque under the Turks. It later fell into decline but was restored in 1956–61 and today serves as an exhibition hall. Look out for the marble doorway inside, which is decorated with bunches of grapes.

➕ *Iraklio 6c* ✉ Odos 25 Avgoustou ☎ (2810) 399228 🕐 Daily 9–1 and some evenings 👋 Free

Agios Petrou Dominikanon

Just to the northeast of the Historical Museum of Crete, the evocative ruins and arches of Agios Petrou lie between the sea and graffiti-splattered modern buildings. The church was built by Dominican monks in the first half of the 13th century and converted into the mosque of Sultan Ibrahim under the Turks. The southern chapel preserves the only 15th-century frescoes in Iraklio, but the church is currently undergoing restoration and is temporarily closed to the public.

➕ *Iraklio 5b* ✉ Odos Sofokli Venizelou ☎ None ❓ Closed for restoration

Agios Titos

Named after the saint who was sent by St Paul to convert the Cretans to Christianity, this building has had a chequered history. The Byzantine church was rebuilt several times after earthquakes, converted into a mosque by the Turks, ruined by another earthquake in 1856, rebuilt again, and, in 1923, reconsecrated to St Titus. The chapel to the left, by the entrance, houses a gold reliquary chalice containing the head of St Titus. This precious relic was taken to Venice for safekeeping when Iraklio fell to the Turks; it was finally returned to its rightful home in 1966 – 300 years later.

➕ *Iraklio 6b* ✉ Odos 25 Avgoustou ☎ (2810) 346221 ⏰ Mon–Sat 8–12, 5–7 ✋ Free 🍴 Cafés and restaurants (€–€€) on Platia Agiou Titou

Istoriko Mouseio Kritis

The Historical Museum of Crete takes up the story where the Archaeological Museum (► 36) leaves off and provides a fascinating insight into the island's turbulent history, from the early Christian era to the 20th century. Slightly away from the city centre, the museum is very pleasant to explore.

The collection starts with an exhibition of artefacts from the Christian period, with emphasis on the Venetian occupation and the Cretan War (1645–1669). This is illustrated by plans, photographs, clear explanations and a highly detailed model of Candia (Iraklio) in 1645. On the same floor, the Ceramics Room illustrates the way in which pottery has evolved over 15 centuries.

The Medieval and Renaissance section displays Byzantine, Venetian and Turkish sculpture, Cretan-school icons, coins, jewellery and a collection of copies of Byzantine frescoes from Cretan churches.

An early painting by El Greco depicts a stormy *View of Mount Sinai* (c1570), with tiny figures of pilgrims climbing up the craggy peak to the Monastery of St Catherine.

The struggle for Cretan independence and the period of autonomy (1898–1908) is illustrated by several portraits of revolutionaries, flags, weapons and photographs. The reconstructions of the studies of the writer Nikos Kazantzakis and Emmanuel Tsouderos, Greek Prime Minister at the time of the

Battle of Crete, take you into the 20th century. The folk rooms on the fourth floor display local crafts and contain a replica of a traditional village home.

www.historical-museum.gr

➕ *Iraklio 5b* ✉ Odos Sofokli Venizelou 27 ☎ (2810) 283219 🕐 Apr–Oct Mon–Sat 9–5; Nov–Mar Mon–Sat 9–3 💶 Expensive

🍴 Nearby waterfront restaurants (€–€€)

Frourio Koules

Guarding the harbour, the mighty Koules fortress was built by the
Venetians in the 16th century on the foundations of an earlier fort.
Various strongholds had occupied the site since the Saracens
arrived in the 9th century, but none as huge and impregnable as
the Venetian structure. Called Rocca al Mare by the Venetians, it
resisted the Turks for 21 years, finally surrendering in 1669. The
winged lion of St Mark – symbol of Venice – decorates three sides
of the fort, the best preserved on the far, seaward side.

There is little to see inside the fort, but the cool chambers and
the walk along the causeway beyond the fortress provide
welcome respite from the bustle of the town. From the top there
are fine views of the harbour, town and the towering peaks of the
Psiloritis in the distance.

Clearly visible across the street from the harbour are the vaulted
chambers of the Arsenali, where the Venetian war galleys were

built and repaired. The shipyards were built between the 13th and the 17th centuries.

✛ *Iraklio 7a* ✉ Iraklio Harbour ☎ (2810) 246211 🕓 Jul–Oct daily 8–7:30; Nov–Jun daily 9–3 (but erratic) ✋ Moderate ❓ Opening hours vary during temporary exhibitions. Upper storey used as an open-air theatre in summer

Krini Morosini (Morozini Fountain)

The central feature of Platia Venizelos, the Morozini fountain was built in 1628 by Francesco Morosini, Venetian Governor of the island. A 16km (10-mile) long aqueduct was built to channel water to it from Mount Giouchtas in the south. The fountain has eight circular basins, decorated with reliefs of nymphs, tritons, dolphins, mermaids, cherubs and mythical creatures. Above, the 14th-century carved lions were incorporated into the fountain and formerly supported a statue of Neptune. Platia Venizelos (familiarly known as Fountain Square) is the tourist centre of Iraklio, and is packed with bustling cafés and restaurants.

✛ *Iraklio 6c* ✉ Platia Venizelos

Mouseio Fysikis Istorias Kritis (Natural History Museum)

Crete's rich panoply of wildlife, plants and landscape are well presented in the University of Crete's Natural History Museum. Recently relocated to an old power station on Iraklio's western seafront, near Dermatas Bay, the museum is still evolving. There are general displays on the island's flora and fauna and there is a particularly important section on fossils relating to Crete and the South Aegean. A major feature is the reconstructed body of the largest mammal that ever lived on Crete during a period nine million years ago and another display deals with earthquake activity. The museum has a strong emphasis on sustainability and environmental protection and this is reflected in an interactive Discovery Centre aimed at young people up to the age of fifteen and covering natural life in various of the island's habitats.

www.nhmc.uoc.gr

✛ *Iraklio 3b* ✉ 5 Odos S Venizelou ☎ (2810) 282740 🕓 Tue–Sun 10–7 ✋ Expensive 🍴 Café (€)

More to see in Iraklio Province

AGIA TRIADA

The small, but appealing Minoan site of Agia Triada (named after its adjacent Byzantine chapel) lies about 3km (2 miles) west of the major site of Phaistos (➤ 54–55) along a narrow surfaced road. The one-time villa that stood here seems likely to have been associated with Phaistos and may have been a summer retreat or small seaport. The sea once reached to the base of the slope on which Agia Triada stands and the remains of a row of shops and a small village beyond the grander villa may indicate seagoing trade of the time. The Harvester Vase and Boxer Vase (now in Iraklio's Archaeological Museum, ➤ 36–37) are just two of the superb Minoan artefacts found here.

✚ 10F ✉ 3km (2 miles) west of Phaistos ☎ (28920) 91360 🕓 Jul–Oct daily 8–7:30; Nov–Jun Tue–Sun 8:30–3 ✋ Moderate 🍽 Café (€) at Phaistos 🚌 Buses only as far as Phaistos, then a 3km (2-mile) walk

CRETAQUARIUM

Best places to see ➤ 38–39.

FODELE

Fodele is the birthplace of El Greco – or it claims to be. Scholars argue that the painter was born in Iraklio. In any event, the village makes a pleasant detour, along a verdant valley of orange and lemon groves.

Over

3

Over the bridge, streets are lined by rustic, flower-decked dwellings. The **El Greco House** is well signposted, and lies about 1km (0.6 miles) from the centre, opposite the Byzantine Church of the Panagia.

✚ 14H ✉ 19km (12 miles) northwest of Iraklio, 3km (2 miles) south of the E75

🍴 Taverna El Greco (€)

🚌 2 per day from Iraklio

Smiti El Greco (El Greco House)

✉ Opposite the Byzantine Church of the Panagia

☎ (2810) 521500

🕐 May–Oct Tue–Sun 9–5

✋ Inexpensive

GORTYS
Best places to see ➤ 42–43.

KNOSSOS
Best places to see ➤ 46–47.

LIMENAS CHERSONISOU
Packed with holidaymakers in pursuit of fun and sun, Limenas Chersonisou and neighbouring Malia make up the biggest tourist area on Crete. The strips of grey sand and pebble are barely sufficient to cope with the crowds, but many visitors opt for sea-view bars anyway. Nightlife centres on the discos, clubs and bars.

A walk around the harbour provides a pleasant break from the bustle, as well as fine views of the mountains towering behind the high-rise blocks. A seaport thrived here in ancient times but only vestiges survive of its ancient splendour. The submerged remains of the Roman harbour are just visible off the headland and, amid the video bars, souvenirs and boutiques on the seafront, you can see the fenced-in fragments of a Roman fish mosaic.

The resort offers a variety of nearby diversions. The **Lychnostatis** (Cretan Open-Air Museum) gives an insight into authentic Cretan life. At Piskopiano's **Museum of Rural Life** workshops and agricultural tools are displayed within an old olive-oil mill. To the east and south of the resort, explore the ever-popular slides and rides of the Star Beach Water Park and the Aquaplus Water Park (➤ 72).

✚ 18H ✉ 28km (17 miles) east of Iraklio 🚌 Regular buses from Iraklio
🍴 Countless bars and tavernas in the centre (€–€€)
Agrotileo Mouseio Limenas Chersonisou (Museum of Rural Life)
✉ Piskopiano (3km/2 miles south of Limenas Chersonisou) ☎ (28970) 23303
🕐 Apr–Oct daily 10–7
Lychnostatis
✉ Limenas Chersonisou ☎ (28970) 23660; www.lychnostatis.gr 🕐 Tue–Sun 9–2 ✋ Expensive

MALIA

To the east of this resort lie the ancient Minoan remains of **Malia Palace.** The ruins are not as spectacular as those of Knossos, but the setting, on a quiet stretch of the coast between the sea and Lasithiou mountains, is rather more impressive. Those who have visited Knossos or Phaistos will recognize the layout around the central court, with storerooms, ceremonial stairways, royal apartments and lustral basin. The origins are similar too. The palace was built in around 1900BC but destroyed by an earthquake in 1700BC. A second palace was built on the foundations, but (unlike Knossos) it was completely destroyed in the unknown catastrophe of 1450BC. Among the many treasures discovered here were an axe head in the shape of a leopard and a sword with a crystal hilt, both of which are now in the Archaeological Museum, Iraklio (► 36).

Archaeologists are continuing to excavate a town which lay around the palace. A 10-minute walk northeast towards the sea brings you to the Khrysolakkos (Pit of Gold), a burial site where priceless jewellery was discovered, including an exquisite gold bee

pendant, also in the Iraklio Museum. The unashamedly brash and rowdy resort of Malia – along with neighbouring Limenas Chersonisou (➤ 94) – is the party capital of the island. Packed with discos, video bars and burger joints, Malia is similar to Limenas Chersonisou, but has a far better beach, with sands stretching a considerable distance to the east. A wide range of water sports, including diving, is available.

✚ 18J ✉ 36km (22 miles) east of Iraklio
🚌 Regular service from Iraklio

Anakforo Malia (Malia Palace)

✉ 3km (2 miles) east of Malia ☎ (28970) 31597 🕐 Apr–Oct Tue–Sun 8:30–7:30, Mon 1–7:30; Nov–Mar daily 8:30–3
💰 Moderate; free on Sun in winter
🍴 Café/bar on premises (€–€€)
🚌 Regular service from Malia and Iraklio

MATALA

Matala made its name in the 1960s when foreign hippies (Cat Stevens and Bob Dylan among them) took advantage of the free accommodation offered by the historic rock caves. Unpopular with both locals and archaeologists, the hippies were evicted long ago. Today Matala attracts tourists of all ages, but it still appeals in particular to independent travellers. The climate is milder than the north coast and sunsets can be enjoyed from the beach tavernas and bars, one of which, Lion's Bar, calls itself the Last Bar Before Africa – true if it wasn't for the island of Gavdos (➤ 167). Matala's main attraction is its sand-and-shingle beach, sheltered between sloping ochre-coloured cliffs which are riddled with man-made caves. The caves range from small hacked-out holes to rooms with carved benches, steps, windows and fireplaces. No-one knows who made the original caves, but they are believed to have been Roman or early Christian tombs. The sands are very crowded in summer. Behind the beach the village now caters almost entirely for tourists, but the resort is still pleasantly free of high-rise buildings, as much of the accommodation is in guest houses. There are boat trips to smaller beaches further south or you can walk over the rocks (about 20 minutes) to Red Beach, named after its reddish-brown sands.

➕ 10F ✉ 70km (43 miles) southwest of Iraklio 🕒 Caves 11:30–7 ✋ Caves free 🚌 Services from Iraklio, Moires and Phaistos

MYRTIA

Myrtia is a pretty place to visit, surrounded by vines and full of flowers and potted plants. It is proud of its connection to the writer Nikos Kazantzakis, and announces the museum at either end of the village in five languages. Kazantzakis' father lived on the central square in a large house which has been converted into a **museum** dedicated to the writer. Best known for his novel, *Zorba the Greek*, Kazantzakis was also a poet, travel journalist and essayist. The museum houses a collection of first editions of his books, costumes from his plays, stills from films of his books, photographs and personal belongings.

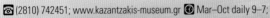 16J ✉ 16km (10 miles) southeast of Iraklio 🍴 Cafés (€) in the square

Nikos Kazantzakis Museum

☎ (2810) 742451; www.kazantzakis-museum.gr 🕐 Mar–Oct daily 9–7; Nov–Feb Sun 10–3 ✋ Moderate

PHAISTOS

Best places to see ➤ 54–55.

TILISOS

Reached off the old Iraklio/Rethymno national road, and set
in the mountains, surrounded by olive groves and
vineyards, Tilisos is home to three Minoan villas dating from
the New Palace period (1700–1450BC). Like Knossos and
Phaistos, which were built at the same time, there are
signs of earlier structures. Excavated in the 20th century,
the villas are referred to as Houses A, B and C, the best
preserved being A (straight ahead as you enter the site)
and C (the house on the left).

The ruins are far less imposing than those of the famous
Minoan palaces, but it is interesting to see where lesser
mortals lived – it is also a delightful, peaceful spot for a
stroll. House A, largest of the villas, has storerooms with
reconstructed *pithoi* (large storage jars), a court with
columns, a lustral basin and stairs which indicate an upper
floor. House C is the most elaborate of the three.

➕ 15J ✉ 10km (6 miles) west of Iraklio ☎ (2810) 226470
🕐 Tue–Sun 8:30–3 💰 Moderate 🍽 Taverna (€) next to the site
🚌 Service from Iraklio

VORI

Set amid olive groves and with views of the mountains, the
old village of Vori is the home of the excellent **Mouseio
Kritikis Ethnologia (Museum of Cretan Ethnology)**, a
past winner of the Best European Museum award
presented by the Council of Europe. Inconspicuously
located in a building near the church, it is a modern
museum with exhibits beautifully laid out behind glass and
informatively labelled. Devoted to traditional crafts and
ways of life in rural Crete, the museum has separate

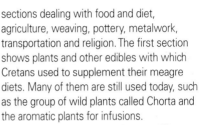

sections dealing with food and diet, agriculture, weaving, pottery, metalwork, transportation and religion. The first section shows plants and other edibles with which Cretans used to supplement their meagre diets. Many of them are still used today, such as the group of wild plants called Chorta and the aromatic plants for infusions.

The weaving section displays 25 different types of baskets made of reed, wild olive, rush, myrtle and other natural materials. The baskets served a variety of purposes, from trapping fish, harvesting sultana grapes and keeping snails to draining cheese. Pottery, made in Crete since Minoan times, includes vessels for raki, vinegar and water, and storage pots for oil, wine, cereals and honey.

✚ 11F ✉ 4km (2.5 miles) north of Phaistos
🍴 Tavernas (€–€€) 🚌 Service from Iraklio

Museum of Cretan Ethnology

☎ (28920) 91110 🕐 Apr–Oct daily 10–6; in winter by appointment ✋ Moderate

HOTELS

AGIA PELAGIA
Out of the Blue Capsis Elite Resort (€€€)
One of Crete's largest and most luxurious complexes, on a peninsula with sandy bays either side. The hotel comprises two main buildings and villa-like bungalows set among beautifully maintained gardens. Facilities include two sandy beaches, indoor and outdoor pools, water sports, fitness centre, shopping arcade, and even a zoo which includes the rare Cretan ibex. The Taverna Poseidon offers 30 different Greek *mezedes*, fresh local fish, music and wonderful views across the bay.

✉ Agia Pelagia ☎ (2810) 811212; www.capsis.gr

IRAKLIO TOWN
Astoria Capsis Hotel (€€)
A civilized and modern hotel close to the Archaeological Museum on the busy Eleftherias Square in the centre of Iraklio Town. There is some noise from the busy streets around the hotel, but it makes up for this with good facilities, including a fourth-floor swimming pool with snack bar, main restaurant and ground-floor Café Capsis. There are 117 air-conditioned rooms and 14 suites.

✉ Platia Eleftherias ☎ (2810) 343080; www.astoriacapsis.gr

El Greco (€)
On a busy shopping street, this is one of the town's most central hotels. There are 90 rooms, of which most could be described as adequate rather than spacious. The public rooms include a snack-bar, cafeteria and breakfast room. As is the case with all of the hotels in Iraklio Town, noise is one of the main drawbacks.

✉ 4 Odos 1821 ☎ (2810) 281071; www.elgrecohotel.gr

Grecotel Amirandes (€€€)
Indulge yourself in the lush garden landscapes of this 5-star resort and spa located at Gouves, 18km (11 miles) east of Iraklio. It has an Olympic-size swimming pool, beach, several restaurants, bar, the Elixir Spa and deluxe rooms, suites and villas.

✉ PO Box 106, GR-711-10, Iraklio ☎ (28970) 41103; www.grecotel.com

Hotel Galaxy Irakleio (€€–€€€)

Excellent first-class hotel, slightly outside the city centre and on the way to Knossos. There are deluxe rooms, executive suites and one Presidential suite, the largest freshwater swimming pool in the city, high-speed internet in all rooms, WiFi in public areas and all the other modern amenities travellers expect today.

✉ Odos Leoforos Dimokratias 75 ☎ (2810) 238812; www.galaxy-hotel.com

Kastro (€)

Don't expect a scenic outlook at this otherwise decent modern hotel. It's in a quiet backstreet close to the town centre and about 0.5km (third of a mile) from the port. Rooms are smart and well maintained and breakfast is included.

✉ Theotokopoulou 22 ☎ (28102) 85020; www.kastro-hotel.com

Lato (€€)

A stylish, well-equipped hotel, close to the old port and Archaeological Museum, the Lato caters for both business and pleasure travellers. Modern, soundproofed guest rooms come with TV, air conditioning, internet access, minibars and balcony; some overlook the fortress by the port. Book in advance.

✉ Epimenidou 15 ☎ (2810) 228103; www.lato.gr

Olympic (€€)

This is a longstanding hotel overlooking the busy area around the Bembo Fountain. The hotel has had a stylish renovation and now has comfortable modern rooms with internet access. Breakfast is included and there's a restaurant and roof garden and an all-day café for drinks and snacks.

✉ Platia Kornarou ☎ (28102) 88861; www.hotelolympic.com

MATALA
Hotel Zafiria (€€)

Matala's largest hotel has 70 rooms and is on the main road in the town centre. Rooms are simple, but all have a balcony facing either the sea or the hills inland. There is a bar and restaurant.

✉ Matala ☎ (2810) 45112; www.zafiria-matala.com

RESTAURANTS

FODELE

El Greco (€)

Pretty setting in the village which, according to the locals, was the birthplace of Domenico Theotokopoulos, known through history as El Greco. The emphasis is on meat, with lamb and chicken on the spit.

✉ Fodele ☎ (28150) 21203 🕙 Daily 11–3, 6–10. Weekends only in winter

IRAKLIO TOWN

Central Park (€)

Essential coffee or drinks right on the edge of the El Greco garden, this popular place draws a stylish local crowd, starts early and keeps going until late. Food options include sandwiches, burgers, pasta, pizzas and finger food.

✉ Arkodeontos 19 ☎ (28103) 46 500 🕙 Daily 8am–1am

Giakoumis (€)

Unfancy local food steams away at this marketside taverna where they start cooking the soup first thing in the morning. If you want the real unvarnished Greek cuisine, this is the place.

✉ Odos Theodosaki 8 ☎ (28102) 84039 🕙 Tue, Wed, Fri 7am–9pm, Thu, Sat 7–4

Ippokampos (€€)

For a true Iraklion experience eat at this busy *ouzerie*, even if you have to wait for one of the pavement tables. Choose several snacks from the tapas-style menu, and keep eating till you're full.

✉ Odos Mitsotaki 13 ☎ (2810) 280240 🕙 Mon–Fri 1–3:30, 7–late

Kirkor (€)

The speciality of this café overlooking the Morozini Fountain is *bougatsa*, the calorific, creamy custard pastry, liberally sprinkled with icing sugar.

✉ Platia Venizelos ☎ (2810) 284295 🕙 Mon–Fri (some Sats) 5:30am–11pm

Kyriakos (€€€)

When locals want to impress their guests, they take them to Kyriakos, long considered Iraklio's best restaurant. There is outdoor seating as well as a dining room, the formal atmosphere softened by lush plants and friendly service. Simply, but beautifully prepared dishes. Reservations essential.

✉ Odos Dimokratias 45 ☎ (2810) 222464 🕐 Daily lunch and dinner

Loukoulos (€€€)

An elegant restaurant on one of Iraklio's prettiest streets, which lures fashionable young locals as well as tourists. The food is Mediterranean with the emphasis on pastas and pizzas. Imaginative, very generous salads and delicious bread.

✉ Odos Korai 5 ☎ (2810) 224435 🕐 Mon–Sat lunch and dinner

Pagopeion (€€)

Popular spot in a pretty setting on Agios Titos square. An old ice factory (*pagopeion* in Greek), it has been converted to a stylish restaurant/café/bar serving breakfast, lunch and dinner. Live or disco music is played until the early hours.

✉ Platia Agios Titos ☎ (2810) 246028 🕐 Daily 10:30am–3 or 4am

Peri Orexeos (€€)

This staunchly Cretan restaurant is small but big-hearted when it comes to good helpings of modern Greek cuisine that include such delights as snails with rosemary and grilled Manouri cheese with tomatoes. Mains include very tasty stir-fried pork with vegetables and white wine.

✉ Korai 10 ☎ (28102) 22679 🕐 Daily 1pm–midnight

MALIA
Petros (€€)

The most pleasant place to eat in Malia is away from the bustling resort in the old town. Petros is one of the several tavernas set on the village square beside the church, and serves solid Greek fare such as *stifado* (beef in tomato sauce).

✉ Platia Agiou Dhimitriou ☎ (28970) 31887 🕐 Daily 5–11pm

MATALA

Lions Restaurant (€€)

Although this is one of several tavernas with an inviting setting right on Matala beach, Lions' menu is more varied than most. Fresh seafood takes top billing. There is also an upstairs open-air bar for drinks and snacks.

✉ Matala ☎ (28920) 45108 🕐 Daily 9am–late

Skala (€€)

You'll find this popular, family-run taverna at the far end of the waterfront, on top of the rocks with wonderful views across the beach. There's fresh fish on the menu and open-air dining on the pretty terrace. A great place to relax and unwind.

✉ Matala ☎ (28920) 45489 🕐 Daily 10am–late

PHAISTOS

Agios Ioannis (€)

Agios Ioannis is an inviting taverna with tables in the garden. It has good home-made fare; the speciality of charcoal-grilled rabbit is recommended.

✉ Matala road, Phaistos ☎ (28920) 31560 🕐 Daily 11–10

SHOPPING

Bookstore Poetry

Directly opposite the Archaeological Museum is this quirky little shop that deals mainly in Greek-language books, but also has a good range of English translations of some of Greece's finest writers. It's fascinating to see T. S. Eliot and W. H. Auden in Greek.

✉ Xsanthoudidou 3, Iraklio ☎ (28102) 86758 🕐 Variable hours

Diktamos

This small, cheerful shop sells a wide range of natural Cretan products, from soaps and sponges to comb honey and spices. Local wine, raki and herbed olive oils are presented in decorative glass bottles.

✉ Museum Square, Iraklio ☎ (2810) 226186 🕐 Daily 9–7

Helen Kastrinoyanni

Opposite the Archaeological Museum, Helen Kastrinoyanni's shop specializes in Cretan handwoven embroideries, rugs, woven linen, jewellery and reproductions of clay figurines which you may well recognize if you have already visited the museum.

✉ Platia Eleftherias 1, Iraklio ☎ (2810) 226186 ⏺ Summer Mon–Sat 8:30–7:30, Sun 11–7; winter shorter hours. Closed Sun

News Stand

Near the Morozini Fountain is this useful newsagent with a wide range of foreign newspapers including *The Times* and *The Wall Street Journal*. It also stocks a small but good collection of paperbacks.

✉ Platia Venizelos ☎ (28102) 20135 ⏺ 8:30am–9:30pm

Planet International

This is the largest bookshop in Iraklio Town and a good source for a wide variety of English-language books, including novels and guidebooks on Crete.

✉ On the corner of Odos Hortatson and Odos Kidonias, behind Platia Venizelou, Iraklio ☎ (2810) 281558 ⏺ Mon, Wed, Sat 8–2; Tue, Thu, Fri 8–2, 5:30–9

ENTERTAINMENT

Café Veneto

A stylish and elegant place for a cup of coffee. Alternatively it is a popular spot for drinks with a fine view over the harbour and the Koules Fortress.

✉ 9 Epimenidou Street, Iraklio ⏺ Daily 10–late
☎ (28102) 27645

Camelot

One of many discos in the late-night resort of Limenas Chersonisou. You won't find many Cretans here but young tourists love it. Good music and dancing.

✉ Agias Paraskevis 10, Limenas Chersonisou ☎ (6944) 314867 ⏺ Mon–Fri 11:30pm–4:30am, Sat–Sun 11:30pm–6:30am

Karouzanos Evening

Excursions are organized to the traditional mountain village of Karouzanos, near Kissamos. The evenings start with a glass of raki, followed by a walk around the village, a drink in a *kafenion* (traditional café) and a typical Cretan-style dinner in a local taverna, with free-flowing wine. The meal is accompanied by Cretan dancing.

Information from: ✉ Kato Karouzana Pediados, Iraklio ☎ (28910) 32404-5

Kazantzakis Theatre

This is an open-air venue for concerts, theatre and dance during Iraklio's summer festival. Some free performances.

✉ Jesus Bastion, near the Oasis Gardens ☎ (2810) 242977 🕓 Jul–Sep; all performances start at 9:30

Lion's Bar

Also known as the Last Bar Before Africa (it would be if it weren't for the island of Gavdos), Lion's Bar has wonderful views of the sunset (and the sunrise). Twenty-one different cocktails, music of all types and impromptu dancing enhance your evening. Meals are served until late.

✉ Matala Beach, Matala ☎ (28920) 45759 🕓 All day and all night until 5 or later. Closed winter

Plateia Korai

Plateia Korai is the liveliest place in the town for an evening drink and is popular with young people. There are several casual bars with tables on the square, serving cocktails and other drinks. International and modern Greek music.

✉ Platia Korai, Iraklio 🕓 Open all day, but liveliest after 9pm

Saloon Bar-Café

If you want to let your hair down and have a wild time, this neon-lit place on the main street is hard to miss. Karaoke nights, music from the 1960s onwards and late-night dancing and partying with an international crowd.

✉ Sofokli Venizelou 198, Limenas Chersonisou ☎ (28970) 23119

Lasithiou Province

This eastern province may not boast the majestic mountains of central or western Crete, but it has plenty of other attractions, both scenic and cultural.

The tourist mecca is Agios Nikolaos, overlooking the beautiful Gulf of Mirampellou. From here the main road snakes its way to Sitia, hub of the eastern end of Crete and a base for the beaches of Vai and Itanos. Further south lie the ancient remains of the palace of Zakros, one of the major Minoan sites on the island. The most dramatic geographical feature of the region is the Lasithiou Plateau, whose flat, fertile fields are ringed by the towering peaks of the Dikti Mountains. The south coast, where plastic greenhouses proliferate, is less scenic than the north, with little development. Ierapetra, the main town, has limited attractions for tourists.

AGIOS NIKOLAOS

From a peaceful little harbour town, Agios Nikolaos has grown
into the most popular resort on Crete. In the Hellenistic era this
was the port for Lato, whose archaeological remains can be seen
in the hills to the west (► 123). The town fell into decline under
the Romans but was later developed by the Venetians, who built
a fort dominating the Bay of Mirampellou (Beautiful View). In 1303
the fort was damaged by an earthquake, then later razed by the
Turks. In 1870 Sfakiots from western Crete settled at the port,
naming it after the Byzantine church of Agios Nikolaos to the north.
The town today may not boast the architectural features and
historic background of Crete's other regional capitals; nonetheless

it is a very picturesque resort with a lively atmosphere that appeals to all ages. Agios Nikolaos' favoured location on its promontory overlooking the blue Gulf of Mirampellou enhances its status as a lively modern Greek town that doubles as a colourful tourist centre.

In the centre of the resort tavernas and cafés cluster around the busy fishing harbour and the deep-water Lake Voulismeni, which is linked to the harbour by a short canal. By day the main activity is strolling around the quaysides, browsing over souvenirs and whiling away the hours over lunch. Public bathing areas leave much to be desired. The small strips of shingle and rock are invariably crowded, but you can walk or bus to the sandy beach of Almiros, 2km (1.2 miles) to the south.

A steep walk up from the port leads to the **Archaiologiko Mouseio (Archaeological Museum).** Dating from the 1970s, this is a modern museum with a small collection of locally found treasures that were previously housed in the Archaeological Museum in Iraklio, and it is well worth a visit. Exhibits are arranged chronologically, from the early Minoan and neolithic period (6000–2100 BC) to the Graeco-Roman era. The emphasis is on Minoan works of art including terracotta figures of deities, Vasiliki flameware vases, seal stones, pottery and jewellery. The prize piece is the early Minoan Goddess of Mirtos in Room II – a stylized, libation vessel in the form of a clay figure (c2500 BC) with a fat body, long skinny neck and tiny head, clasping a water jug. In the same room the beautiful

gold jewellery in the form of ribbons, leaves and flowers came from the island off Mohlos (▶ 124). The late-Minoan 'larnakes', or clay sarcophagi, in the next room were also used as bath tubs – one of them contains the bones of two bodies. In Room IV, a rare late-Minoan infant burial tomb is displayed as it was found. In the last room the grinning 1st century AD skull, bearing a wreath of gold olive leaves, was discovered at the Potamos necropolis near Agios Nikolaos. The silver coin found in its mouth is the fare for the ferry ride to the Underworld, across the mythical River Styx.

The tiny **Mouseio Laographiko (Folk Museum)** near the tourist office is devoted mainly to folk art. Among the local crafts on display are finely woven and embroidered textiles, woodcarvings, weapons, ceramics and Byzantine icons. Agios Nikolaos' modest **Municipal Art Gallery** is housed on the second floor of the charming 19th-century Damanakis mansion. Changing exhibitions of artwork are staged throughout the year and often feature quite challenging works by contemporary Greek artists.

🚩 20J 🚌 Regular service to Iraklio, Malia, Limenas Chersonisou, Sitia and Ierapetra 🚢 Services to Sitia, Piraeus, Milos, Santorini, Karpathos, Kassos, Kas, Rhodes and other islands

ℹ️ Odos Akti I Koundourou 21A ☎ (28410) 22357

Archaeological Museum

✉️ Odos Palaioiogou 68 ☎ (28410) 24943 🕐 Tue–Sun 8:30–3 ✋ Moderate; free on Sun and national hols from Nov–Mar 🍴 Taverna Aouas (€€)

Folk Museum

✉️ Ground floor of Harbour Master's Office, opposite the bridge ☎ (28410) 25093 🕐 Apr to mid-Oct daily 10–2, 5–7 ✋ Moderate

Municipal Art Gallery

✉️ Oktobriou 28 ☎ (28410) 26899 🕐 Daily 11–2, 6–9 ✋ Free

a walk in Agios Nikolaos

This walk begins at the harbour in the centre of the resort.

From the harbour walk up the tamarisk-lined Odos Roussou Koundourou, one of the two main shopping streets. Take the first street to the left, Odos Sfakianaki.

Towards the far end of Odos Sfakianaki there are splendid views of the Gulf of Mirampellou. The marina below was constructed in 1994.

At the end of the street, overlooking the marina, follow a pleasant seaside promenade anti-clockwise round a headland with splendid views of the Gulf and plenty of wayside seats for a picnic, to reach the town beach of

Kitroplatia. Turn right past the beach and follow the waterfront to the harbour.

Enjoy a drink in one of the waterside cafés. The boats and cruisers moored here offer fishing, swimming and glass-bottom boat trips, excursions to Spinalonga Island (▶ 119) and evening tours of the bay.

Make for the bridge on the west corner of the harbour and the small Folk Museum (▶ 112). Walk up the steep Odos Palaiologou for a visit to the Archaeological Museum (▶ 111), then retrace your steps down to the lake on your right.

The 64m (210ft) deep Lake Voulismeni, encircled by fishing boats and flanked by cliffs on its western side, was originally believed to be bottomless. In 1867 it was linked to the harbour by a channel and cleared of its stagnant waters. Today it is a tourist magnet, the lakeview cafés luring customers with their tempting range of exotic ices and cocktails. For the best views climb the steps at the far side, beyond the Café du Lac.

Distance 1.8km (1 mile)
Time 2 hours (including sights)
Start Point Harbour **End Point** Lake Voulismeni
Lunch Taverna Pelagos (€€) ✉ Korakai and Katehaki
☎ (28410) 25737

DIKTEON ANDRON (DIKTAEAN CAVE)

According to myth, the Diktaean Cave was the birthplace of Zeus. His father, Kronos, who feared being overthrown by a son, consumed the first five of his offspring. However, when Zeus was born, his mother Rhea presented Kronos with a stone instead of a baby and Zeus was concealed inside the cave, protected by warriors and fed by a goat. As a small child, he was then transferred to the Idaean Cave (► 148).

The actual cave is very impressive, but the site is highly commercialized and crowded. Beware of greedy car park attendants and costly donkey rides. Non-slippery shoes are essential. There are now concrete steps and lighting to help you negotiate the 65m (213ft) descent, but unless you are hiring a guide you may want to bring a torch to better examine the cave's natural features more closely.

The cave is a kilometre (0.6 miles) up from the car park, via a steep path or by a longer paved walkway. An expensive donkey ride is the easy alternative. If you happen to arrive before the tour crowds, the dark cave, with its stalactites and stalagmites, is highly atmospheric. Down in the depths, the venue of ancient cult ceremonies, guides point out the chamber where Zeus was born, and features such as the face of Kronos and a stalagmite in the shape of Rhea and Zeus. Altars, idols and a large number of pottery and bronze votive offerings were found within the cave, some dating back to a pre-Minoan era.

🔒 18K ✉ Psychro, Lasithiou ☎ (29770) 364335 🕐 Daily 8–6:45; 8:30–3 in winter 💷 Moderate 🍴 Tavernas (€€) at the car park or in the village 🚌 Limited service from Iraklio and from Agios Nikolaos

ELOUNDA AND SPINALONGA

Thanks to a stunning setting and a choice of luxury hotels Elounda is one of Crete's most desirable resorts. It lies north of Agios Nikolaos, reached by a road which snakes its way above the Gulf of Mirampellou, then drops scenically down to the centre of the resort. Life here focuses on the cafés and tavernas around the boat-filled harbour, and the long sandy beach stretching beyond.

Coming into the resort from Agios Nikolaos, a sharp right turning off the main road leads to a causeway linking Elounda to the Spinalonga peninsula. From here you can see the submerged remains of Venetian salt pans. The sunken remnants of the Graeco-Roman city state of Olous lie towards the end of the causeway to the right of the peninsula. The remains are barely visible but the peninsula is a pleasant place to stroll, with coastal paths and birdlife. A path beside the Canal Bar (just across the bridge) leads to a Byzantine mosaic featuring fish and geometric designs – this is all that remains of an early Christian basilica.

Elounda's luxury accommodation, including Crete's finest hotel (Elounda Beach ➤ 70) is situated away from the centre, off the road going south to Agios

Nikolaos. In peaceful surroundings, the hotels have their own private beaches and take full advantage of the glorious views over the gulf.

The rocky island of Spinalonga, reached by ferries, lies off shore and is dominated by its Venetian fortress, built in 1579 to protect the port of Elounda. A resistance movement operated here and it was not until 1715, 46 years after the Turkish conquest of the rest of Crete, that the fort finally surrendered. In 1903 the island was turned into a leper colony, where conditions were cruel and prison-like until the construction of a hospital in 1937. Twenty years later the colony was closed and the patients were taken to an Athens hospital. Today the island is uninhabited and the fortress and town are in ruins.

✚ 20J ✉ 7km (4 miles) north of Agios Nikolaos 🍴 Ferryman Taverna (€€) on the waterfront 🚌 Regular service to Agios Nikolaos ❓ Boats to Spinalonga island daily in season, every 30 minutes, 9–4:30

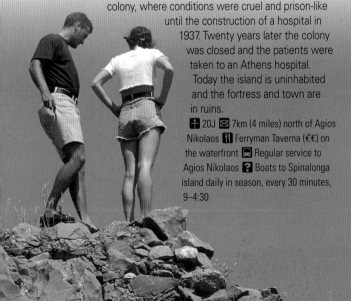

GOURNIA

The ruins of the Minoan town of Gournia sprawl over the hillside, just off the main Agios Nikolaos–Sitia coastal road. The site is remarkably extensive, and the excavations revealed a thriving Minoan trading town of winding alleys lined by tiny houses, workshops, a marketplace and, on top of the hill, a palace, believed to have belonged to the local ruler or governor. The palace was originally three storeys high, with pillars, courtyards, storerooms and apartments. In relation to Knossos and Phaistos this was something of a mini palace, and the people who lived in the town were probably quite humble in comparison to those of the more famous establishments. Like the other Minoan sites of Crete, Gournia was destroyed in 1450BC, then virtually abandoned. Many finds are housed in the Archaeological Museum in Iraklio (► 36) and a few in the museum at Sitia (► 128). If the site is closed, there is a good view from the lay-by next to the entrance track.

✚ 20K ✉ 19km (12 miles) southeast of Agios Nikolaos ☎ (28410) 24943
🕐 Apr–Oct 8:30–7; Nov–Mar 8:30–3
🖐 Moderate 🍴 Fish tavernas at Pachia Ammos (€–€€), 2km (1.2 miles) 🚌 Service to Agios Nikolaos and Sitia

IERAPETRA

Ierapetra is the most southerly town of Europe, enjoying mild winters and many months of sun, and even in mid-winter people bathe in the sea. Agriculture is the mainstay, with off-season vegetables produced in the ugly plastic greenhouses which surround the town.

Both a workaday town and tourist resort, Ierapetra has a bustling, slightly scruffy centre, a pleasant seafront promenade, a

long grey sand beach and an old Turkish quarter with a mosque and fountain house. Architecturally it is uninspiring, and it has little to show of its past importance as a flourishing trading centre. Under the Dorians this was a leading city of Crete, and during the Roman occupation it saw the construction of temples, theatres and other fine buildings. Evidence of its more recent history is the Venetian fortress guarding the harbour. Built in 1212, and refortified by the Turks, this is used today for cultural events during July and August.

The **Archaiologiko Mouseio (Archaeological Museum)** in the centre has a small collection of local finds from Minoan to Roman times. They are not labelled or described, but an English-speaking custodian can usually help. The museum's showpiece is a Minoan larnax, or clay coffin, from Episkopi, north of Ierapetra, which is decorated with lively hunting scenes.

In high season boats leave from the quayside every morning for the island of Yaidhouronisi (or Chrysi Island, ➤ 67) – a popular excursion for those who want to escape the bustle of the town.

✚ 20L ✉ 35km (22 miles) south of Agios Nikolaos 🚌 Regular service to Agios Nikolaos, Iraklio and Sitia

Archaeological Museum

☎ (28420) 28721 🕐 Tue–Sun 8:30–3 👖 Moderate

KRITSA

Clinging to the slopes of the Dikti Mountains, Kritsa is a large hill village with fine views over the valley. Crafts are the speciality and shops are hung with rugs, embroidery and other home-made (and foreign) products.

So close to Agios Nikolaos and also home to the Panagia Kera (► 52), this is a popular destination for tour coaches, but despite inevitable commercialism, the village retains much of its charm as a working hill community.

➕ 19K ✉ 10km (6 miles) southwest of Agios Nikolaos 🚌 Several a day from Agios Nikolaos ❓ Re-enactment of Cretan weddings in August

LASITHIOU PLATEAU

The most visited inland region of Lasithiou, the plateau has a spectacular setting, encircled by the Diktaean peaks. Watered by the melting snow from the mountains, the soil is highly fertile, yielding potatoes, cereal crops, vegetables and fruit. Traditionally the land was irrigated by canvas-sailed windmills – the familiar symbols of Lasithiou – but these have gradually given way to the more efficient (if considerably less picturesque) diesel pumps. A few of the originals survive, and there is a row of ruined stone windmills at the Seli Ambelou Pass which heralds the plateau on its northern side. A circular road skirts the plateau (► 132), passing through small villages with their simple tavernas and craft shops. To avoid the tour crowds at the Diktaean Cave (► 116), arrive very early in the morning or leave it until the early evening.

➕ 18J ✉ Southwest of Agios Nikolaos 🍴 Taverna Kronio, Tzermiadho (€) 🚌 Buses make a circular tour of the plateau, stopping at all villages

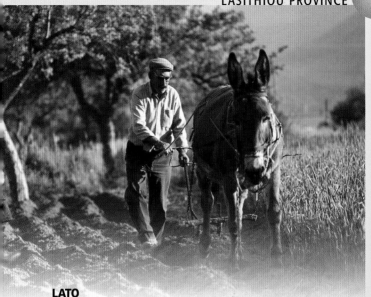

LATO

The remains of this Dorian town (7th–3rd century BC) occupy a magnificent site, spread on a saddle between two peaks above the Kritsa plain. Relatively few visitors come here, favouring instead the more ancient Minoan sites; but the views alone, encompassing sea and mountains, are worth the visit. The layout of Lato is somewhat simpler than that of the Minoan sites and the extensive ruins, rising in tiers, are notable for the massive stone blocks used in their construction including the entrance gateway, the guard towers, the deep workshops with their wells, the olive presses and the corn-grinding querns. A stepped street with houses and workshops leads up to the central agora – the meeting place and cult centre – with a shrine and a deep rainwater cistern. A broad stairway leads up to two council chambers, lined with benches, and two archive rooms. A second stairway leads to a raised terrace with the remains of a temple and altar and a view of the ruined temple on the southeastern hill.

✚ 19J ✉ 3.5km (2 miles) north of Kritsa, 10km (0.6 miles) west of Agios Nikolaos ⏱ Tue–Sun 8:30–3 💷 Free 🍴 Tavernas in Kritsa (€–€€) 🚌 Buses from Kritsa

MAKRYGIALOS

With one of the best beaches on Crete's southeast coast, the fishing village of Makrygialos and its sister village Analipsi is a small but growing resort. Hotel development along the main road hides its charms, but head down to the waterfront for a delightful view of its curving sandy beach lined with pleasant tavernas where fresh fish is always on the menu. The shallow water is warm and great for children.

22K 24km (15 miles) east of Ierapetra Bus service from Ierapetra and Sitia

MOHLOS

From the main E75 between Agios Nikolaos and Sitia, a minor road snakes down to the fishing village of Mohlos, a peaceful place, with seaside tavernas and a pebble beach. Excavations on the offshore island – once joined to the mainland – revealed the remains of what is believed to be a Minoan harbour town. Finds included ancient seal stones and tombs containing precious vases. An inexpensive trip to the island can be made with one of the local fishermen (ask at one of the tavernas and negotiate a price).

21J 40km (25 miles) east of Agios Nikolaos None

MONI TOPLOU

Square and solid, the monastery of Toplou lies isolated in the barren hills east of Sitia. Built in the 14th century, it was fortified to resist pirate attacks and named after a large cannon (*toplou* in Turkish) which was used against invaders. Today it is one of the richest monasteries in Crete. Geared to tourism, the complex may have lost some of its charm as a working monastery, but it certainly merits a visit, particularly for the icons and delightful cobbled courtyard overlooked by three tiers of monks' cells.

The most notable of the many icons in the church is the remarkably detailed Lord Thou Art Great (1770), by Ionnis Kornaros. Beyond the church are engravings, icons and a display about the role which the monastery played against the Turks during the Cretan struggle for independence and during World War II.

🔂 23J ✉ 16km (10 miles) east of Sitia ☎ (28430) 61226 🕐 Daily 9–1, 2–6 👣 Moderate 🍴 Café/snack bar (€) 🚌 Bus service from Sitia then 3km (2-mile) walk from the main road

NEAPOLI

A pleasant provincial town and former capital of Lasithiou, Neapoli makes an obvious starting point for an excursion to the Lasithiou Plateau (➤ 122). Few tourists visit the town, but if you are passing by it is worth stopping at one of the cafés or tavernas in the main square to sample the speciality of the town, *soumadha*, a sweet drink made of almonds. A small museum on the square houses crafts and a handful of local archaeological finds.

🔢 19J ✉ 21km (13 miles) northwest of Agios Nikolaos 🚌 Regular service from Iraklio and Agios Nikolaos

PALEKASTRO

Close to the coast and surrounded by olive groves, Palekastro makes a useful base for tourists wanting to explore the sandy beaches, archaeological sites and other attractions at the eastern end of the island. Expanding rapidly, the village has simple hotel accommodation, numerous rooms to rent, a handful of tavernas and bars and even its own tourist office. About 1.5km (just over a mile) from the village, near the south end of Chiona beach, lie the partially excavated remains of Roussolakos, one of the largest Minoan towns discovered. Excavations are still in progress and the site – mainly of interest to specialists – is open to the public. Artefacts from the site are displayed in the archaeological museums of Sitia and Iraklio. There are good sandy beaches to the south of Palekastro, and between the village and Vai to the north. On this stretch of the coast, Kouremenos beach is a good place for windsurfing.

www.palaikastro.com

🔢 24J ✉ 18km (11 miles) east of Sitia ✋ Roussolakos free 🚌 Services from Sitia, Vai and Kato Zakros

ℹ Tourist office, Palekastro ☎ (28430) 61546

PANAGIA KERA

Best places to see ➤ 52–53.

SITIA

The most easterly town in Crete, at the end of the national highway, Sitia feels quite remote. Both a working port and tourist resort, it is a pleasant, leisurely place, particularly around the taverna-lined quayside and the older streets above the harbour.

The town dates back to Graeco-Roman times, possibly even as far back as the Minoan era, but it was under the Venetians that the port had its heyday. Today it is essentially modern, with buildings set in tiers on the hillside. The only evidence of Venetian occupation is the fortress above the bay, reduced to a shell by the Turks, but used now as an open-air theatre. Sitia's long sandy beach, popular with windsurfers, stretches east from the town, followed by the parallel coastal road.

The **Archaiologiko Mouseio (Archaeological Museum),** just out of the centre, has a good collection of

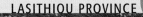

Minoan art, with useful explanations in English. Particularly interesting is the section devoted to Zakros Palace (► 130), with decorated vessels, urns, cooking pots, a wine press and a collection of clay tablets with the rare Linear A script. In the entrance hall pride of place goes to the ivory statuette of a young man (*c*1450) discovered at Palekastro. The **Folk Museum,** up from the harbour, has a collection of traditional crafts, including baskets for carrying grapes, and bedspreads and rugs coloured with dye from indigenous plants.

🚦 23J 🖂 70km (43 miles) east of Agios Nikolaos 🍴 Kastro (€€), on the harbour
🚌 Services from Agios Nikolaos, Iraklio and Ierapetra

Archaeological Museum

🖂 Odos Piskokefalou 3 ☎ (28430) 23917
🕐 Tue–Sun 8:30–3 ✋ Moderate

Folk Museum

🖂 Odos Kapetan Sifi 28 ☎ (28430) 22861
🕐 May–Oct Mon–Sat 9:30–1:30 (also Tue and Thu 6–8) ✋ Inexpensive

VAI BEACH

Backed by a plantation of rare date palms, the tropical-looking Vai beach lies at the northeastern tip of the island. The remote location is no deterrent and the lovely sandy bay is invariably crowded in summer. To see it at its best you must come early in the morning or off-season. Formerly frequented by backpackers, who stayed overnight on the sands, the beach is now strictly regulated, with a camping ban, car park charges and an extensive range of beach facilities.

🕂 24J 🖂 9km (5.5 miles) north of Palekastro 🖐 Car park charges
🍴 Taverna (€€) on the beach 🚌 Service to Palekastro and Sitia

ZAKROS PALACE

Part of the appeal of the Minoan palace of Zakros is the remote valley setting by the coast, seemingly far removed from civilization. However, in Minoan times this was a major centre, linked to a port (now submerged), trading with Egypt

and the Middle East. It wasn't until the 1960s that a Greek professor, Nikolaos Platon, discovered the palace and its archaeological treasures, their quantity and quality suggesting a highly affluent community.

For an overall view of the setting and layout, start at the upper town; then climb down to the lower level and central court. From here, explore the ceremonial hall, a small banqueting hall and a cluster of other rooms, then cross to the royal apartments. The south side of the central court is bordered by workshops, and in the southeast corner excavators discovered 3,500-year-old olives preserved in water at the bottom of a jar. Treasures from the palace are housed in the Archaeological Museum at Iraklio (➤ 36) and Sitia's museum.

🚏 23K ✉ Kato Zakros ☎ (28430) 26897 🕐 Apr–Oct daily 8–5; Nov–Mar Tue–Sun 8–3 🎟 Moderate; free on Sun in winter 🍴 Maria, Kato Zakros (€) 🚌 Twice a day in summer

a drive around Lasithiou Plateau

The tour starts from Neapoli but can also be approached from Agios Nikolaos or the north coast. Take non-slip shoes and a torch for the caves.

Follow the sign for Lasithiou from the main square in Neapoli. The road twists its way scenically up through the mountains.

Stop at the café at Zenia for a break from the bends and a breathtaking view of the Diktaean peaks.

Continue up through villages where locals sell wine, raki and honey by the roadside.

After about 27km (17 miles), the plateau comes suddenly and spectacularly into view. Stop by the roadside to look down on to the flat plain, encircled by soaring mountains.

After the village of Mesa Lasithiou, turn right at the road junction for Tzermiado (signposted to Dzermido).

Signed from the main road, the Kronio Cave (also known as the Cave of Trapeza) was used as a burial site from prehistoric times. Around 1km (0.6 miles) from the parking area, in summer guides can show you the way.

Continue along the road encircling the plateau. At the junction at Pinakiano go straight on, following signs for Psychro. Beyond the village of Plati, follow signs for the Diktaean Cave.

This is Crete's most famous cave (➤ 116), the so-called birthplace of Zeus.

Continue around the plateau. At Avrakontes, where the road branches, take the left branch.

At Agios Georgios there is a small folk museum, signed from the village centre (summer only) and at Agios Konstantinos the full circle of the plateau has been completed. Turn right to return to Neapoli.

Distance 83km (51 miles)
Time 6–7 hours, including stops and lunch
Start/End Point Neapoli ✚ 19J
Lunch Taverna Kronio (€) ✉ Tzermiado ☎ (28440) 22375

HOTELS

AGIOS NIKOLAOS
Hotel Creta (€)
Clean and comfortable studio rooms, all with kitchenettes, make this unpretentious hotel at the heart of Agios Nikolaos an excellent option. The quiet location on the high ground to the east of the harbour is a bonus, as are the views from the upper floors.
✉ Sarolidi 22 ☎ (28410) 28893

Istron Bay Hotel (€€€)
This secluded hotel, 13km (8 miles) east of Agios Nikolaos, has a cliff-hanging setting above a glorious small bay. There are 145 sea-view rooms in local style, three restaurants (the hotel is well-known for its cuisine), open-air pool, tennis, beach bar, water sports, fishing trips and organized day and evening activities. Despite the size, it is family run and has a friendly atmosphere.
✉ 721 00 Kalo Khorio ☎ (28410) 61347; www.istronbay.gr

Minos Beach Art Hotel (€€€)
See page 71.

Sgouros Hotel (€)
The main advantage of this modern hotel is its location by the beach. There is no restaurant but plenty of tavernas nearby.
✉ Kitroplatia, Agios Nikolaos ☎ (28410) 28931;
www.sgourosgrouphotels.com

ELOUNDA
Elounda Beach Hotel (€€€)
See page 70.

PALEKASTRO
Hotel Hellas (€)
This modest and inexpensive family-run hotel is in the centre of the village. The restaurant/café is popular with locals.
✉ Palekastro ☎ (28430) 61240; www.palaikastro.com/hotelhellas
🚌 Services to Sitia, Vai and Kato Zakros

RESTAURANTS

AGIOS KONSTANTINOS, LASITHIOU PLATEAU
Dikti (€)
Unpretentious roadside café with a menu including roast meats, moussaka and salads. The owners also sell embroidery and linen.
✉ Agios Konstantinos, Lasithiou ☎ (28440) 31255 🕐 Daily 8–6. Closed winter

AGIOS NIKOLAOS
Ariadne (€€€)
This fairly expensive restaurant is on the east side of the harbour, one of the best in a scrum of eating places. Justly popular, it is run by a friendly family whose cooking lifts the ordinary menu.
✉ Akti Koundourou ☎ (28410) 22658 🕐 Daily 12–11 in season

Du Lac (€€–€€€)
Long established and popular, the Du Lac is right on the lakeside. It has an excellent menu of fish and seafood dishes among a general menu of Cretan specialities.
✉ Omirou ☎ (28410) 23783 🕐 Daily 9–midnight

Itanos (€€)
Close to Platia Venizelos, up from the port, this is a welcome change from the more commercialized waterfront restaurants. Locals come for genuine Cretan fare and wine from the barrel.
✉ Odos Kyprou 1 ☎ (28410) 25340 🕐 Daily 10–10; lunchtime is best

Pelagos (€€€)
Save this smart taverna for a special occasion. It's in a neoclassical building with a courtyard. The emphasis is on fish and seafood. Try the mussel *saganaki* or the delicious red mullet with herbs. Meat and pasta dishes are also available.
✉ Odos Koraka 11 ☎ (28410) 25737 🕐 Apr–Oct daily 12–12

Zygos (€–€€)
A well-located café-restaurant tucked away on the north side of the lake with fine open views across the town. Ideal for morning

coffee in the sun or for tasty offerings such as octopus in olive oil or a tasty seafood platter for two.

✉ Odos E Antistaseos 1 ☎ (28410) 82009 🕓 Daily 9–midnight

ELOUNDA
Ferryman Taverna (€€)

The Cretan menu here is a cut above the usual fare, with more elaborate dishes such as pork cooked with bacon, mushrooms and garlic in a wine sauce. Try rusk-like Cretan bread.

✉ Waterfront, Elounda ☎ (28410) 41230 🕓 Apr–Oct daily 10am–late

ISTRO
Meltemi (€€€)

This stylish restaurant at the Istron Bay Hotel is open to non-residents and has lovely views over the bay. The restaurant has won awards for its cuisine and wine list. Perfect for a special treat.

✉ Istron Bay Hotel, Istro ☎ (28410) 61303 🕓 Apr–Oct Mon–Wed and Fri–Sat 7–10:30pm

KATO ZAKROS
Maria (€)

Simple fish taverna on a delightful pebble beach, near the remains of Zakros Palace. Fresh fish such as bream, snappers and mullet are usually available.

✉ Kato Zakros, Sitia ☎ (28430) 93316 🕓 Mid-Mar to end Jun, Sep–Oct Tue–Sun 8–3; Jul–Aug daily 8–6

MAKRYGIALOS
Faros (€€)

Fresh fish is assured at this friendly waterfront restaurant, run by a family of fishermen for nearly 40 years. Eat at outdoor or indoor tables; the little bar next door is decorated with old family photos.

✉ Waterfront, Makrygialos ☎ (28430) 52456 🕓 Daily lunch and dinner

Kavos (€€)

The fresh seafood and Cretan specialities change daily at this beachside taverna. It has its own bakery, and the excellent wine comes from the grandfather's vineyard.

✉ Waterfront, Makrygialos ☎ (28430) 51325 🕐 Daily lunch and dinner

MOHLOS
Mesostrati (€–€€)

Mesostrati is an unpretentious place where the emphasis is on good Cretan food without frills. Local cheese *saganaki* in filo pastry with peppers, tomatoes and herbs is a great starter and fish dishes are always well prepared.

✉ Mohlos ☎ (28430) 94170 🕐 10am–late

PALEKASTRO
Elena (€)

This is a taverna of great character, offering Cretan specialities such as rabbit cooked in wine, *briam* (aubergines and courgettes), cheese pies and stuffed vine leaves. Wine comes from the barrel and there are home-made sweets and ice creams.

✉ Palekastro ☎ (28430) 61234 🕐 Apr–Oct daily mid-morning to 11pm

SITIA
Cretan House (€€)

The large outdoor terrace is along the waterfront near the beach. Inside, it is charmingly decorated with a re-creation of a Cretan house. Good Greek and Cretan specialities and fresh fish.

✉ Odos Karamanli 10 ☎ (28430) 25133 🕐 Daily 10am–late

Mixos (€€)

Set back from the harbour, this is where you'll find the locals dining out. Good-value Cretan dishes and charcoal-grilled fish and meat, with heady wine from the barrel to complement the food.

✉ Odos Vinzetzos Kornarou 117 ☎ (28430) 22416 🕐 Daily 10am–late

TZERMIADO, LASITHIOU PLATEAU
Kronio (€)

This is the oldest restaurant on the plateau. Authentic fare includes *stifado*, lamb with white artichokes (spring only), *dolmades* and cuttlefish with spices. Delicious cheese and vegetable pies are served as starters or as a snack.

✉ Tzermiado, Lasithiou ☎ (28440) 22375 🕓 Daily. Closed winter

SHOPPING

AGIOS NIKOLAOS
Ceramica

Nic Gabriel keeps the spirit of traditional Greek forms alive with his handmade copies of ceramics from museums all over Greece.

✉ Odos Paleologou ☎ (28410) 24075 🕓 Daily 9:30am–11pm. Closed winter

Kera

Multiple doorways lead into this Aladdin's cave of gifts and souvenirs selling everything from icons to jewellery, fabrics to pottery.

✉ Odos Akti Koundourou 8 ☎ (28410) 22292 🕓 9am–11pm

ELOUNDA
Petrakis Icon Workshop

Artists Yiorgia and Ioannis Petrakis create beautifully painted icons using traditional materials and methods on Elounda's main street.

✉ Odos A Papandreou 22, Elounda ☎ (28410) 41669; www.greek-icons.com 🕓 Apr–Oct daily 10am–11pm; phone for winter hours

ENTERTAINMENT

AGIOS NIKOLAOS
The Lato

Agios Nikolaos' summer culture-fest sees a colourful programme of theatre, music and dance staged at various venues.

Molo

This ultramodern café-bar, on the terrace above the eastern side of the harbour, is the nighttime haunt for Agios Nikolaos' fashion conscious. Great cocktails and drinks go well with House music and Greek sounds into the early hours. It's also ideal for coffee and snacks by day.

✉ Odos Akti Koundourou 6 ☎ (28410) 26250 🕓 Daily 8am–5am

Rethymno Province

**Rethymno is the smallest and
most mountainous of Crete's
four provinces. To the east it is
bordered by the towering
peaks of the Psiloritis range,
to the west by the Lefka Ori
or White Mountains. Between the
two lies the beautiful green Amari
Valley, where mountain hamlets seem
lost in time. On the north coast the main
attraction is the delightful historic
town of Rethymno.**

Rethymno

Sandy beaches stretch either side of the provincial capital, and the
coast to the east is built up with a long ribbon of tourist
development. South-coast development is restricted by the wild
coastline of cliffs and headlands, and some bays are accessible
only on foot or by dirt track. Agia Galini and Plakias are – for the
moment – the only two resorts developed for package holidays.
The main cultural attractions are the famous monasteries of Arkadi
and Preveli.

RETHYMNO TOWN

Rethymno was a town of little significance until the 16th and 17th centuries when it prospered under the Venetians. Following the fall of Constantinople, many Byzantine scholars sought refuge here and the town became an important intellectual and cultural centre. In 1646 it came under Turkish rule, which lasted 250 years. The old quarter retains much of its Venetian and Turkish character and the town is still regarded as the 'intellectual capital' of the island. Throughout the year there are numerous music, theatre and art events at various venues.

The dominant feature of the town is the mighty Venetian fortress, built to defend the city against pirate attacks. To the east lies the harbour, where the waterside fish tavernas are a magnet for tourists. The narrow, pedestrianized alleys of the old town are ideal for strolling. Down virtually every street there are fascinating architectural details to admire, such as

ornately carved Venetian doorways and arches, the Turkish overhanging wooden balconies and the minarets and domes. Tiny shops are crammed with objets d'art, craftsmen sell leather or jewellery, grocery stores are stocked with herbs, spices and raki.

The town has a wide sandy beach, backed by a palm-lined promenade and tavernas, hotels and cafés. The sands are packed in summer, but there are quieter beaches with cleaner waters to the east and west.

✚ 8C

Archaiologiko Mouseio (Archaeological Museum)

Occupying the former Turkish prison at the entrance to the

fortress, this is now a modern, well-organized museum of Minoan and Graeco-Roman finds from the Rethymno region. Especially noteworthy are the grave goods and decorated sarcophagi from the late-Minoan period, some of them embellished with hunting scenes.

✚ *Rethymno 2a*
✉ Fortetza ☎ (28310) 54668 ⏰ Tue–Sun 8:30–3 💶 Moderate

Fortetza (Venetian Fortress)

At the far end of the promontory, above the town, the Venetian fortress was built in 1573–86 to stem the fearsome Turkish attacks on the city. Believed to be the largest Venetian fort ever built, it was designed to protect the entire population of the town. When the Turks attacked in 1646, the Venetian troops took cover here, along with several thousand townspeople; but after a siege of just 23 days, the fortress surrendered. Today the outer walls are well preserved, but most of the buildings were destroyed by earthquakes or by bombs in World War II. Inside the walls the dominant feature is a mosque built for the Turkish garrison, now restored. Only ruins survive from the garrison quarters, the governor's residence, powder magazines and other buildings, but the atmosphere is evocative and there are fine views. Plays and concerts take place here during the summer months.

✚ *Rethymno 1a* ✉ Odos Katechaki ☎ (28310) 28101 🕐 Tue–Sun 9–6; longer hours in summer 👋 Moderate 🍴 Café (€)

Kentro Sigkronis Ekastikis Dimiorgeas Rethimnis (Centre of Contemporary Art)

This modern art centre is also known as the L Kanakakis Gallery. The stylish whitewashed galleries on two floors host temporary exhibitions of modern painting, sculpture and other media, mainly by Greek artists. It also has a collection of Greek art, including 70 paintings by Lefteris Kanakakis, a local artist.

www.rca.gr

✚ *Rethymno 3b* ✉ Odos Chimarras ☎ (28310) 52530 🕐 Apr–Oct Tue–Fri 9–1, 7–10, Sat and Sun 11–3; Nov–Mar Tue–Fri 10–2, 6–9, Sat–Sun 11–3 👋 Moderate

Mouseio Istorias Kai Laikis Technis (Historical and Folk Museum)

The museum is in a restored Venetian house near the Neratzies Mosque. The galleries house a charming collection of crafts from local homes, including fine embroidery, lace, basketware, pottery, knives and agricultural tools. Explanations, translated into English, accompany displays of bread-making techniques, Greek needlework and other traditional rural crafts.

✚ Rethymno 2b ✉ Odos Vernardou ☎ (28310) 23398 🕐 Mon–Sat 9–2, 6–8; Wed, Fri 9–2 in winter ✋ Moderate 🍴 Cafés and tavernas in Platia Petihaki (€–€€)

Palaiontologiko Mouseio (Museum of Paleontology)

Housed in the renovated Mastaba Mosque/Veli Pasha Mosque, this small but fascinating collection is under the wing of Athen's

prestigious Goulandris Natural History Museum and describes Crete's geology and palaeontology through a series of displays with interpretations in Greek and English. The Mosque is of great architectural interest in its own right and has nine domes and the oldest surviving minaret in Rethymno.

✚ Rethymno 1c, off map ✉ Mastaba ✉ (28310) 23083 🕐 Mon–Sat 9–3 ✋ Moderate

Temenos Nerantze (Neratzies Mosque)

South of the Rimondi Fountain, the three-domed mosque's finest feature is its soaring minaret. Originally the Church of Santa Maria, it was converted into a mosque by the Turks shortly after their defeat of Rethymno. The minaret was added in 1890 and, prior to closure for safety reasons, afforded splendid views of the town. Today the mosque is a music school and concert hall.

✚ Rethymno 3b ✉ Odos Vernadou 28–30 ☎ (28310) 22724 🕐 Closed to public except for concerts 🍴 Tavernas in Platia Petihaki (€–€€)

More to see in Rethymno Province

AGIA GALINI

At the foot of the Amari valley, with houses, hotels and apartments stacked up on the hillside, Agia Galini has grown from a remote fishing village into a big tourist resort. The narrow streets of the centre lead down to a harbour of fishing boats and pleasure cruisers and are packed with tavernas, bars and souvenir shops. It is a friendly, cheerful place, but it can become claustrophobic in high season and there is an alarming amount of further construction on the way. The resort beach of stony, dark grey sand to the east of the village is not ideal but there are boats to the more attractive beaches of Agios Georgios and Agios Pavlos to the west, and daily cruises to the lovely sandy beaches of the Paximadia Islands, 12km (7 miles) off shore.

✚ 10F ✉ 54km (33 miles) southeast of Rethymno 🍴 Onar (€€)
🚌 Services to Iraklio, Rethymno, Phaistos and Matala

ANOGIA

Lying below the peaks of the Psiloritis range, Anogia is
the last village before the Idaean Cave, and the main
starting point for the hike up to the summit (see Oros
Psiloritis, ➤ 148). The village is best known for its crafts,
particularly handwoven blankets, rugs, wall hangings and
embroidery, all of which you will see on display in the
shops. Women at their looms give the village the air of a
long-established settlement, but while old traditions
survive, all the buildings are new. During World War II,
General Kreipe, Commander-in-Chief of the German
forces, was kidnapped by partisans and hidden in
Anogia, before being removed from Crete. In retaliation
the Germans destroyed the entire village, apart from
the church, and killed many of the menfolk.

✚ 11D ✉ 35km (22 miles) west of Iraklio ⓘ A couple of simple
tavernas (€) in the village 🚍 Service from Iraklio and Rethymno

BALI

On the north coast, east of Rethymno, Bali is a small but growing
resort of rocky coves and tiny sand and shingle beaches. The one-
time fishing village is now built up with hotels and apartments, and
life here centres primarily on tavernas, bars and discos. Paradise
Beach (also known as Evita Beach) is the best place to swim, but
the beach is incredibly crowded in summer. Apart from water
sports and boat trips to Rethymno there is not a great deal to do
here, but Bali is situated roughly half-way between Iraklio and
Rethymno, and only 2km (1.2 miles) from the national highway, so
there are plenty of opportunities for excursions.

✚ 10C ✉ 30km (19 miles) east of Rethymno ⓘ Harbourside tavernas
(€–€€) 🚍 2km (1.2 miles) from bus stop for service to Iraklio and Rethymno

MONI ARKADIOU

Best places to see ➤ 48–49.

MONI PREVELI
Best places to see ➤ 50–51.

OROS PSILORITIS (MOUNT PSOLOREITIS)

At 2,456m (8,055ft), Mount Psoloreitis, or Mount Ida, is the highest point on Crete. From Anogia (➤ 147) a winding road through barren, mountainous terrain leads to the Nida Plateau at the foot of the mountain. Near the end of the road, by the taverna, a path leads up to the Idaiki Spilia (Idaean Cave), a contender, along with the Diktaean Cave (➤ 116), for the title of birthplace of Zeus. Excavations in the 1880s yielded bronze shields from the 9th and 8th centuries BC, suggesting that the cave was a post-Minoan cult centre. You can walk down into the cave, but it is fairly shallow with no dramatic natural rock formations. The path to the summit of Mount Psoloreitis also starts at the taverna – a gruelling 7–8 hour return trip.

✚ 10E ✉ 17km (11 miles) south of Anogia to base of mountain

PLAKIAS

A rapidly expanding resort, Plakias' main asset is its setting, with a long sweep of beach surrounded by steep mountains. It is a fairly low-key place, with hotels and apartments, a couple of discos and several beach tavernas with lovely views of the sunset. The beach of shingle and coarse sand is rather exposed, but there's a better one at Damnoni, reached by car or a 30-minute walk.

🞤 8E 🖂 22km (17 miles) southwest of Spili 🚌 Regularly to Rethymno

PREVELI BEACH

The beautiful sandy cove at the mouth of the Kourtalioti Gorge can be reached by boat or by a steep and demanding walk from Moni Preveli (► 50). It is also known as Palm Beach, after the date palms that line the banks of the River Megapotomos, which flows into the sea at Preveli. Idyllic off-season, the beach fills to overflowing with boatloads of tourists in the summer.

🞤 8E 🖂 38km (24 miles) south of Rethymno 🚢 Day trips from Plakias and Agia Galini

SPILAIO MELIDONIOU (MELIDONI CAVE)

Mythical home of Talos, the bronze giant who guarded the coasts of Crete, the Melidoni Cave has some splendid stalactites and stalagmites. But it is not so much the natural beauty of the cave as its tragic history that has earned it fame. In 1824 around 370 of the villagers, mostly women, children and the elderly, hid here from the Turks. Troops laid siege to the cave but the villagers refused to surrender and shot two of the enemy. In retaliation the Turks blocked the entrance of the cave, trying to suffocate the Cretans. Then they lit fires at the cave mouth, asphyxiating everyone inside. An ossiary in one of the chambers still contains the victims' bones, and an annual commemoration service is held in the local church.

🞤 10C 🖂 4km (2.5 miles) northeast of Perama, a short drive or 30 minutes' walk from the village of Melidoni ☎ (28340) 22046 🕓 Apr–Nov daily 9–6:30/7 ✋ Moderate 🍴 Bar by the cave (€)

in the Amari Valley

a drive

Dwarfed on the east side by the Psiloritis massif, the Amari valley offers glorious views.

From Rethymno head east on the old national highway, turning right at the sign for Amari. At the village of Agia Fotinis go straight on. Where the road divides, take the left branch, signposted Thronos.

Thronos has a lovely church with medieval frescoes and a Byzantine mosaic pavement. (Ask locally for the key if the church is locked.) Beyond the church a path leads up to the ruins of the ancient city of Sybrito.

Beyond Thronos, at a junction by a bus shelter keep straight on. At the next junction, beside a factory, turn right, signposted Scholi Asomaton. Go straight on at the next junction. At the T-junction turn left, signposted Fourfounas. Just past a taverna turn right, signposted Amari. At a T-junction turn right to Amari.

Amari has wonderful valley views and some faded frescoes in the Church of Agia Anna.

Retrace your route to the junction at the taverna and turn right following signposts for Fourfounas. Go through Nithavris and take the road east to Zaros (24km/15 miles).

An attractive mountain village, Zaros is famous for its springs. Stop for lunch at one of the tavernas serving trout.

Return towards Rethymno, this time taking the road on the west side of the valley, to reach Gerakari.

Gerakari is famous for its cherry trees, and you can buy bottled cherries and cherry brandy in the village.

Back at Agia Fotinis, turn left to return to Rethymno.

Distance 165km (102 miles)
Time With stops and lunch allow a full day
Start/End Point Rethymno ✚ 8C
Lunch Taverna Votomos (€€) ✉ Zaros ☎ (28940) 31302

HOTELS

AGIA GALINI
Minos Hotel (€)

Great sea views from the front of this pleasant family-run hotel enhance the clean and comfy rooms. Other rooms overlook the entrance to the resort. There are convenient, shared kitchen areas.

✉ Agia Galini ☎ (28320) 91292; www.minos.agiagalini.com

PANORMO
Club Marina Palace (€€€)

Half the rooms at the Club Marina Palace are aimed at families, and there are childcare facilities like babysitting, an early supervised family dinner, baby phones and pushchairs available. For adults, the Elixir Thalasso Spa might be of more interest, and there are several pools and restaurants, though for a break you can easily visit the fishing village of Panormo nearby.

✉ Panormo ☎ (28340) 51610; www.grecotel.com

RETHYMNO TOWN
Atelier (€)

Tucked away below the walls of the Fortetza, there are a few rooms above the owner's pottery (➤ 155). They are immaculate with an updated traditional Cretan feel: exposed stone walls and wood-beamed ceilings. Each room has cooking facilities.

✉ Himaras 27, Rethymno ☎ (28310) 24440; www.frosso-bora.com

Fortezza (€€)

Centrally located, and close to the old fort, this stylish hotel in the centre of town has its own swimming pool and garden courtyard. All rooms have air conditioning and balconies.

✉ Odos Melissinou 16 ☎ (28310) 55551

Ideon (€€)

Good-value hotel, well placed for the centre of the city and the Venetian harbour. Built in the 1970s, it offers 95 modern rooms with air conditioning, a swimming pool and a restaurant.

✉ Platia Plastira 10 ☎ (28310) 28667

Minos Mare (€€€)
Large, modern hotel standing on the sand-and-shingle beach of Platanias, 5km (3 miles) from Rethymno. Ideal for all ages, with pools, gym, sauna, evening entertainment and children's facilities. Guests can also use the facilities of the sister hotel, the Minos, 3km (2 miles) away.

✉ Platanias, Rethymno ☎ (28310) 50388; www.minos.gr

Mythos Suites Hotel (€€–€€€)
The Mythos Suites Hotel, in the centre of Rethymno and ideal for the old town, has seven studio apartments for one or two people, and eight suites sleeping up to four persons. It's a small, boutique-style hotel with very helpful service and all the rooms and suites have phones, satellite TV, internet access and a fitted kitchenette.

✉ Platia Karaoli, Rethymno ☎ (28310) 53917; www.mythos-crete.gr

Palazzo Rimondi (€€€)
See page 71.

Palazzo Vecchio (€€)
See page 71.

Plaza Spa Suites (€€€)
Right on the beachfront at the eastern end of Rethymno, the Plaza Spa Suites have 45 individually decorated 1- and 2-bedroom apartments and 39 deluxe maisonettes. There's also a taverna on site, two outdoor and one indoor swimming pools and a spa.

✉ Ari Velouhioti 61, Perivolia ☎ (28310) 51505; www.classicalhotels.com/plazaspasuites

RESTAURANTS

AGIA GALINI
Onar (€€)
The main attraction here is the splendid harbour and sea views from the roof-garden restaurant. Wide range of Greek dishes, as well as home-made pizzas, pasta and fresh fish.

✉ Agia Galini ☎ (28320) 91288 ◷ Easter–end Oct all day every day

RETHYMNO TOWN

Alana (€€€)

A courtyard venue in the old town, the Alana offers traditional Greek cuisine with both Mediterranean and international influences. Dishes with flair include pork with plums and pistachio nuts.

✉ Salaminos 15 ☎ (28310) 27737 ⏱ Daily, dinner

Avli (€€€)

It is well worth splashing out for a meal in this elegant restaurant within an historic Venetian manor house. Signature dishes include grilled octopus and fava with caramelized beetroot and lamb with greens in egg-lemon sauce. The wine list is unusually varied and gives useful explanations of Cretan and Greek wines. Delightful courtyard for outdoor meals. Reservations are recommended.

✉ Odos Xanthoudidou 22 ☎ (28310) 26213 ⏱ Daily 11–3, 7–11

Cavo d'Oro (€€€)

One of the best of the many fish restaurants clustered round the tiny Venetian harbour in Rethymno, the Cavo d'Oro is as popular with locals as with visitors. It has fresh fish daily, and unusual dishes as well as a good list of Cretan wines.

✉ Nearchou 42 ☎ (28310) 24446 ⏱ Daily noon–late

Fanari (€)

Avoid the tourist traps. Do what Greek visitors do and wander towards the fortress and a quieter stretch, which offers sea views and more authentic Greek cuisine in informal places like the Fanari, with an excellent *meze* menu.

✉ Kefalogiani 16 ☎ (28210) 54849 ⏱ Daily 11–11

O Gounos (€)

In the old town, this is a lively place on summer evenings when the family play folk music. Wholesome home-cooking with Cretan specialities.

✉ Odos Koronaiou 6 ☎ (28310) 28816 ⏱ Daily, lunch and dinner

Palazzo (€€€)

Thanks to the enticing harbour setting and choice of delicious fresh fish and seafood, this is one of the most expensive restaurants in town. Save it for a special occasion and reserve a rooftop table.

✉ Rethymno Harbour ☎ (28310) 25681 🕒 Daily, lunch and dinner

La Rentzo (€€€)

There is plenty of atmosphere in this old Venetian interior. It is on the pricey side but is smart and friendly, and makes a good spot for a candlelit dinner. Tables are also laid outside in summer. International and Greek dishes include lamb in honey sauce. Order in advance for special dishes, especially for fresh fish.

✉ Odos Radamanthous 9 ☎ (28310) 26780 🕒 May–Oct lunch and dinner; Nov–Apr dinner only (6–1)

Sunset Taverna (€€)

This taverna lives up to its name, enjoying splendid sunsets from the west side of the Fortetza. Reliable Greek food, longer-than-average wine list and tables by the sea.

✉ Periferiakos ☎ (28310) 23943 🕒 Apr–Oct daily, mid-morning to late

Veneto (€€€)

Gourmet dining in the restaurant of the chic Veneto hotel, where the chef prepares wonderfully tasty versions of Cretan specialities, with a focus on organic ingredients such as salmon mille-feuille with avocado and *myzithra* cheese. Extensive wine list.

✉ Epimenidou 4 ☎ (28310) 56634; www.veneto.gr 🕒 May–Oct daily 6pm–midnight

SHOPPING

Atelier Pottery Workshop

Housed on the ground floor of Atelier rooms (➤ 152) is the workshop of Frosso Bora, where she creates and sells a range of charming and reasonably priced ceramic ware.

✉ Himaras 27, Rethymno ☎ (28310) 24440; www.frosso-bora.com 🕒 Apr–Oct daily 9–9

Avli (Raw Materials)

Run by the Avli Restaurant (► 154) this delicatessen has an awesome selection of the best Cretan delicacies, including olives, olive oil, cheese, honey, raki and wines from Crete and other Greek wineries.

✉ Arabatzoglou 38–40, Rethymno ☎ (28310) 58228; www.avlirawmaterials.gr 🕐 Daily 9am–10pm. Reduced hours in winter

Nikos Siragas Wood Art

The authentic and talented artist Nikos Saragas works at his lathe in his Rethymno gallery on most summer evenings. His work is functional but also creative.

✉ Petalioti 2, Rethymno ☎ (28310) 23010; www.siragas.gr 🕐 Apr–Oct Mon–Sat 10:30–2:30, 6–10:30

ENTERTAINMENT

Figaro

Cool sounds and relaxed company are the deal at this café-bar close to the imposing minaret of the Neratze Mosque.

✉ Vernarou 21, Rethymno ☎ (28310) 29431 🕐 Sun–Thu 10am–3am, Fri, Sat 10am–4am

Fortezza, Rethymno

Every summer, concerts, theatrical performances, ballet, recitals, traditional dance and song are performed at the Venetian fortress.

✉ Odos Katechaki, Rethymno ☎ (28310) 29148 🕐 Mid-Jul to mid-Sep

Fortezza Club

Not to be confused with the Fortezza, above, this old-established club aimed mostly at the smart local market is terrific fun.

✉ Nearchou 14, Rethymno ☎ (28310) 55493; www.fortezzaclub.gr 🕐 Daily midnight–dawn

Neratzies Mosque Concerts

The splendid Neratze Mosque is now a music school where public concerts are staged in summer.

✉ Vernardou 28–30, Rethymno ☎ (28310) 22724

Chania Province

The most westerly province in Crete, Chania has no great archaeological sites but it provides some of the most spectacular scenery on the island. Views are dominated by the majestic peaks of the Lefka Ori (White Mountains), snow-capped for six months of the year. On the south coast the mountains drop to the Libyan Sea, leaving little space for development.

Chania

Compared to the flatter north coast, the south is sparsely populated, with just a handful of villages nestling below the mountains and a couple of holiday resorts with beaches. Spectacular, walkable gorges are a feature of the White Mountains, particularly the Samaria Gorge, which is the second most popular attraction in Crete. On the north coast the historic town of Chania, which has the island's most beautiful harbour, makes a delightful base.

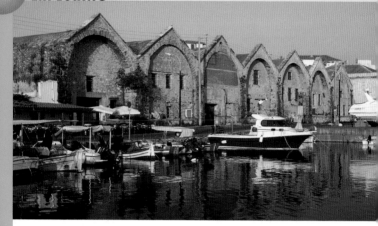

CHANIA TOWN

The ancient city of Kydonia, inhabited since neolithic times, became the most important settlement in Crete after the destruction of Knossos. The town fell into decline under the Arabs, but during the Venetian occupation (1290–1646) La Canea, as it was renamed, became 'the Venice of the East'. Following the Turkish occupation, which was from 1646–1898, Chania was made capital of Crete and remained so until 1971.

Chania is not only the best base for exploring western Crete, it is arguably the island's most appealing town. Beautifully set below the White Mountains, it has a lively harbour, a maze of alleys and a string of beaches nearby. Strolling is the most pleasurable activity, either along the harbourfront, or through the streets of the old town, where Venetian and Turkish houses have been elegantly restored. Along the narrow alleys are such charming features as old portals and overhanging balconies, as well as enticing hole-in-the-wall craft shops and cafés.

The real magnet is the outer harbour, with its faded, shuttered houses, and its crescent of cafés and tavernas overlooking the water. This is where the locals come for their early evening *volta*. The inner harbour, overlooked by Venetian arsenals, is another focal point, with fishing boats, pleasure craft and tavernas. Chania may be picturesque, but there are often too many tourists

crowding the narrow streets. To appreciate its
beauty, visit early or later in the day.

✚ 5B

Archaiologiko Mouseio (Archaeological Museum)

The Church of St Francis was the largest church to
be built in Chania during the Venetian era, and its spacious vaulted
interior makes a handsome setting for the archaeological
discoveries from excavations in the region. The exhibits span the
period from late neolithic to Roman occupation,
and greatly assist in adding a human dimension
to the ancient sites of the area.

The majority of artefacts date from the late
Minoan era and include pottery, weapons, seals,
decorated clay tombs *(larnakes)* and tablets
inscribed with Linear A and B scripts.The
Graeco-Roman section is represented by a
collection of sculpture and glassware, leading up
to three fine Roman mosaics, which were
discovered in villas in Chania, displayed at the far
end of the church.

The little garden beside the church features a
damaged Lion of St Mark, and a beautifully
preserved ten-sided Turkish fountain, dating from
the period when the church was converted by
the Turks into a base of a minaret.

✚ *Chania 2b* ✉ Odos Khalidon 21 ☎ (28210) 90334
🕐 Summer Mon 1–7:30, Tue–Sun 8:30–7:30; winter
Mon 1–5, Tue–Fri 8:30–5, Sat–Sun 8:30–3 💶 Moderate
🍴 Tavernas in Odos Khalidon or on the harbour (€–€€€)

Chania Limani (Chania Harbour)

Best places to see ➤ 44–45.

Mouseio Nautiko (Naval Museum)

Tracing Crete's sea trade and maritime warfare, the Naval Museum is housed in the restored Venetian Firkas Tower guarding Chania's harbour. Most of the exhibits here are models of ships, ranging from the simple craft of the Copper Period (2800BC) to submarines built in the 1980s. The collection also contains marine weapons and instruments, historical documents, a model of the Venetian town of La Canea and, on the first floor, an exhibition devoted to the World War II Battle of Crete in 1941. Beyond the gate, the strategically sited bastion commands impressive views of the harbour, the Venetian lighthouse and the domed Mosque of the Janissaries (built in 1645, following the Turkish conquest). It was here, at the Firkas fortifications, that the Greek flag was first raised on Crete in November 1913.

✚ *Chania 2b* ✉ Fort Firkas, Akti Koundourioti ☎ (28210) 91875 ⊕ Daily 9–4; 10–2 in winter ✋ Moderate

Vizantino Mouseio (Byzantine Museum)

Chania's newest museum is in a small, renovated church on the western side of the fortress. Its displays incorporate a range of Byzantine artefacts, including mosaics, sculptures and jewellery, as well as the usual collection of icons. A highlight is the icon of St George slaying the dragon, at the far end of the musem. It was painted by Emmanuel Tzanes Bouniales (1610–90), one of the foremost artists of the Cretan school of icon painters. Particularly outstanding are the brightly coloured fragments of 11th-century wall frescoes. The San Salvatore collection, in a well-lit side gallery, includes a beautiful display of glass-bead necklaces, jewellery, crosses, ceramics, Byzantine coins and a rare bronze lamp from the 6th and 7th centuries. There are also some fascinating post-Byzantine artefacts, such as the curious horned mask from 16th–17th century Chania town.

✚ *Chania 1a* ✉ Odos Theotokopoulou 82 ☎ (28210) 96046 ⊕ Tue–Fri 8:30–7, Sat–Sun 8:30–3 ✋ Moderate; free on Sun in winter

a walk around Chania

Start at the Naval Museum (► 161), which is situated on the west side of the Old Harbour.

With the water on your right, walk along Akti Koundourioti to reach the attractive Platia Talo, where there is a striking memorial to the ferry Iraklio, which sank off Crete in 1966 with much loss of life. From here turn inland down Odos Theotokopoulou, a picturesque street with old Venetian houses and craft shops. At the end, turn left down Odos Zambeliou and at the main square (the harbour is to your left) turn right along Odos Halidon.

Odos Halidon, lined with shops, is the tourist hub of Chania. On the right is the Archaeological Museum

(► 159) and just beyond it, in the courtyard of the Catholic church, the small Folk Museum. On the other side of the road lie the old Turkish baths, now occupied by a shop, and a large square, overlooked by Chania's unremarkable cathedral.

Take the second left for Odos Skridlöf, a narrow alley packed with leather stalls and, at a crossing, go straight on along Odos Tsouderon, lined with modern shops. Pass the entrance to Chania's Market (► 74), then cross Daskalogiani, then turn left down the narrow Kallistou and go through a leafy enclave, keeping left where it narrows even more, to emerge on Platia 1821.

The Platia is over-looked by Agios Nikolaos, a former mosque with a soaring minaret.

Go diagonally left across the square and then turn right down Daskalogiani.

At the waterfront you can walk along the jetty to the lighthouse, or turn left to return to the Old Harbour, passing the Mosque of the Janissaries.

Distance 2.5km (1.5 miles)
Time 2–3 hours including sightseeing
Start/End Point Venetian Harbour ✚ *Chania 2a*
Lunch Dinos (€€€) ✉ Akti Enoseas 3, Inner Harbour
☎ (28210) 41865

More to see in Chania Province

ELAFONISI

The semi-tropical beach of Elafonisi is one of the finest in the whole of Crete, with its pink-tinged sands and vivid turquoise waters. The beach is located in a remote part of the southwest of the island and visitors who wish to reach it by car face a long drive and many hairpin bends.

However, it is no longer the undiscovered and idyllic haven it used to be – there are now several restaurants, small hotels, rooms to rent and, in high season, tourist boats and buses crammed full with eager day trippers.

A more peaceful alternative to the main resort beach is the tiny island of Elafonisi, just offshore, which is reached by wading knee-deep through the turquoise waters. Here there is another small idyllic beach, where the waters are clear, shallow and ideal for children.

✚ 2D ✉ 6km (4 miles) south of Chrysoskalitisas
🚌 Once a day from Chania ⛴ Ferries from Palaiochora

FALASSARNA

As you wind down the hillside to the west coast, Falassarna's magnificent sweeping beach comes into view, its crescent of pale sands, lapped by azure waters, stretching round to Cape Koutri in the north.

Named after a local mythical nymph, Falassarna is also the site of an ancient city,

the remains of which can be seen 2km (1.2 miles) north of the beach. (Follow the track for 1.5km/1 mile beyond the last building.) Among the scattered remnants of the Hellenistic city-state are a 'throne' carved out of the rock, tombs, quarries, towers, water cisterns and the ruins of a number of houses and storerooms.

The remains centre around the harbour basin, its location some 100m (328ft) inland showing clear evidence of the gradual shifting of the island. In the distant past, probably around 365BC, Crete's west coast was uplifted by 6–9m (20–30ft), while parts of eastern Crete were submerged, including the sunken city of Olous (➤ 118). Excavations of the ancient city are still in the early stages, and only a small portion of the harbour has been unearthed.

More remains lie at the top of Cape Koutri, site of the acropolis. Close by, the less appealing – but economically necessary – plastic greenhouses produce off-season vegetables for export to mainland Greece.

✚ 2B ✉ 8km (5 miles) northwest of Platanos ✋ No charge to see the ruins
🍴 Two tavernas above the beach (€–€€)
🚌 Two per day from Chania

FARAGI IMBROU (IMPROS GORGE)

North of Hora Sfakion (Chora Sfakion), the Impros Gorge is a small-scale version of the famous Samaria Gorge (➤ 40). Not quite as spectacular but with similar scenery, it is far more peaceful than Samaria. The gorge is about 8km (5 miles) long, and the walk takes from 2 to 3 hours, either uphill from the coast east of Hora Sfakion, or downhill from Impros village at the beginning of the gorge. At the end you either have to walk to Hora Sfakion, catch a bus or wait for a taxi in Komitades. The walk can only be made between May and October since winter torrents render the gorge impassable.

🚌 6E ✉ 54km (33 miles) southeast of Chania 🚻 Free 🍴 Café (€) in Impros
🚌 Service from Chania and Hora Sfakion ❓ Sturdy footwear and drinks recommended

FARAGI SAMARIAS (SAMARIA GORGE)

Best places to see ➤ 40–41.

FRANGOKASTELLO

The great square fortress, formidable from a distance, is actually no more than a shell. It was built by the Venetians in 1340 in an attempt to subdue the rebellious Sfakiots and pirates who were attacking Crete. In 1770 the Sfakiot rebel leader, Daskaloyiannis, was forced to surrender to the Turks here, and in 1828, during the Greek War of Independence, the Greek leader, Hatzimichali Dalianis, along with

several hundred Cretans, died defending the fort against the Turks. According to the locals, on the anniversary of the massacre in mid-May their ghosts appear at dawn and march around the walls.

Below the fortress there is excellent swimming and snorkelling from the long sandy beach, and there are tavernas, shops, rooms to rent and even a disco. Less crowded beaches lie to the east and west.

🞤 6E ✉ 17km (11 miles) east of Hora Sfakion ✋ Free 🚌 Limited service to Hora Sfakion and Plakias

GAVDOS

A remote island between Crete and the shores of northern Africa,

Gavdos is the southernmost point in Europe. A few families eke out a living here and there are some rooms to rent and a couple of basic tavernas. The landscape is somewhat desolate and sunbaked, but for those prepared to walk there are some beautiful, unspoilt beaches. Ferries (which can take several hours if the seas are choppy) arrive at Karabe; from here you walk for half an hour to the nearest beach or climb for an hour up to Kastri, the main village on the island. Sometimes visitors can get transport from locals meeting the ferries.

🞤 6F ✉ 48km (30 miles) south of Hora Sfakion 🍴 Limited choice (€) 🛳 Ferries from Palaiochora and Hora Sfakion

a walk through the Samaria Gorge

Start at the tourist pavilion at the head of the gorge. Hikers should come equipped with sturdy footwear, sunhat, sunscreen and refreshments (there are drinking points and streams along the gorge but no food).

Take the stairway known as the xiloskala *(wooden stairs) which drops steeply, descending 1,000m (3,280ft) in the first 2km (1 mile).*

This section of the walk is particularly hard on the knees and ankles. The first landmark is the tiny Church of Agios Nikolaos, shaded by pines and cypresses.

The path narrows as you reach the bottom of the gorge (4km/2.5 miles from the start). In summer the river is reduced to a mere trickle.

The half-way point, and a good spot for a picnic, is the abandoned village of Samaria. The inhabitants were rehoused when the area became a national park. To the east of the gorge lies the small 14th-century Church of Ossia Maria, containing original frescoes. The church gave its name to the village and gorge.

Follow the narrowing trail between towering cliffs, crossing the river at various points. Continue walking until you see a small church on the left.

Beyond the sanctuary built by the Sfakiots, you can see ahead the famous *sideroportes* or Iron Gates. The corridor narrows to a mere 3m (10ft), the towering walls either side rising to 300m (984ft).

Beyond the gates, the path opens out and you walk down the valley to the coast.

At the old abandoned village of Agia Roumeli, a drinks kiosk is a welcome sight.

Continue to the modern coastal village of Agia Roumeli where tavernas, the cool seawater and the ferry back to civilization await.

Distance 16km (10 miles)
Time 5–7 hours 🕐 May to mid-Oct (mid-Apr to Oct weather permitting)
Start point Omalos Plain, 43km (27 miles) south of Chania ✚ 4D 🚌 Service from Chania
End Point Agia Roumeli ✚ 4D 🚢 Ferries to Hora Sfakion (Chora Sfakion), where there are buses back to Chania. Check times of the last boats and buses. Guided tours available through travel agents.
Lunch Tavernas at the top of the gorge and in Agia Roumeli (€–€€); a picnic is recommended for the gorge.

GEORGIOUPOLI

This north-coast resort was named in honour of Prince George, who became High Commissioner of Crete in 1898, after the Turks were forced to recognize the island's right to autonomy. The fishing village is now a well-established resort, with hotels, rooms to rent and a huge sweep of beach, but despite ongoing construction, it is still a relatively peaceful and relaxed place. The eucalyptus trees which shade the large central square are watered by the River Almyrou, which flows into the sea at Georgioupoli. To explore the river, its birdlife, crabs and turtles, you can hire pedaloes or canoes from the little chapel which sits at the end of the causeway. The sandy beach stretches for several kilometres to the east, but beyond the causeway, the strong currents make swimming conditions dangerous.

✚ 7D ✉ 22km (14 miles) west of Rethymno 🍴 Tavernas on the main square (€–€€) 🚌 Service to Rethymno and Chania

HORA SFAKION (CHORA SFAKION)

In the 16th century this was the largest town on the south coast, with a population of 3,000, but rebellions during the Turkish occupation left Hora Sfakion largely impoverished, and what remained of the town was destroyed by bombs in World War II. Today it is no more than a small resort and ferry port, its main appeal the setting between the mountains and the crystal clear waters of the Libyan Sea. The small pebble beach is not ideal but you can take boats or walk to Sweetwater Beach, which takes its name from the freshwater springs seeping from beneath the rocks. The beach is a popular spot for nudist campers.

In high season the seaside tavernas of Hora Sfakion cater for boatloads of hungry hikers coming from the Samaria Gorge, waiting for buses back to Chania. The town has always been the capital of this mountainous, remote region and Sfakiots, as the locals are known, are traditionally a proud and independent people. The region was a centre of resistance during the fight for Cretan independence and continued this heroic tradition in World War II, sheltering Allied troops after the Battle of Crete.

🕇 6E ✉ 67km (42 miles) south of Chania 🍴 Seafront tavernas (€–€€)
🚌 Service to Chania and Plakias 🚢 Ferries to Agia Roumeli (Samaria Gorge), Sougia, Palaiochora and the island of Gavdos

KISSAMOS

This is a pleasant coastal town, still retaining some of its Cretan character but offering little of architectural interest. Few tourists stay here but there are a couple of hotels and some rooms to rent, many of them by the beach. In the town's main square, the Archaiologiko Mouseio (Archaeological Museum) is closed indefinitely for restoration. The best places to eat are the tavernas on the seafront, where you can also sample a glass of the locally produced red wine.

🕇 2B ✉ 40km (25 miles) west of Chania 🍴 Papadakis (€) 🚌 Services to Falassarna, Hora Sfakion, Chania and Palaiochora

KOLIMBARI AND MONI GONIAS

At the foot of the Rodopou peninsula, Kolimbari is an unspoilt coastal village, where local life goes on undisturbed by the few tourists who stay here. The beach is pebbly but the waters are crystal clear and there are splendid views over the Gulf of Chania.

About 1km (0.6 miles) north of the village the Moni Gonias has a delightful coastal setting. Founded in 1618, it has been rebuilt several times but the Venetian influence can still be seen in some of the architectural features. The small church contains some wonderfully detailed little icons from the 17th century along the top of the iconostatis, as well as votive offerings and other treasures. The most precious icons, dating from the 15th century, are housed in the museum, along with reliquaries and vestments. If the church and museum are closed, ask one of the monks to show you round. He will probably also point out the Turkish cannon ball lodged in the rear wall of the church.

✚ 3B ✉ 23km (14 miles) west of Chania ☎ (28240) 22518 🕐 Sun–Fri
8–12:30, 4–8; Sat 4–8 (shorter hours in winter) 🎫 Free 🍴 Seafront fish
tavernas (€–€€) in Kolimbari 🚌 Service to Kolimbari from Chania and
Kissamos

LOUTRO

The only way to get to this
delightful, car-free village is on
foot or by boat. It is a tiny,
remote place, with white cubed
houses squeezed between
towering mountains and the
Libyan sea. There are half a
dozen tavernas, a simple hotel,
rooms to rent and some villas,
but the majority of visitors are
day trippers coming on ferries
from Hora Sfakion and Agia Roumeli. The pebble beach is not ideal
but you can bathe from the rocks or hire canoes to explore
offshore islets, coves and beaches. There are also boat trips to the
sandy cove of Marmara and to Sweetwater Beach.

✚ 5E ✉ 5km (3 miles) west of Hora Sfakion (Chora Sfakion) 🍴 The Blue
House (€) ⛴ Ferry service to Hora Sfakion and Agia Roumeli

MALEME

The resort of Maleme is part of the long ribbon of modern
development west of Chania. But it is for its role in World War II
that this part of the coast is best known. It was at the Maleme
airstrip that the Germans first landed in their invasion of 1941, the
Allied forces retreating from 'Hill 107' above the airstrip. The
Germans occupied this strategic target – but not without
casualties. Today 'Hill 107' is the location of the German War
Cemetery, where nearly 4,500 Germans are buried.

✚ 4B ✉ 16km (10 miles) west of Chania

MONI CHRYSOSKALITISAS

In a remote location at the southwest tip of the island, the whitewashed nunnery perches on a promontory above the sea. It was founded in a cave in the 13th century, but the present building dates from the mid-19th century and contains little of interest to the average tourist. Of the 200 sisters who used to live here, just one and a monk remain. For centuries Moni Chrysoskalitisas, its barrel roof a distinctive landmark, was a refuge for victims of shipwrecks on this remote and treacherous coast. The name 'Chrysoskalitisas' means 'Golden Steps', and was taken from the stairway of 90 steps leading from the nunnery down to the sea. According to legend, one of the steps is made of pure gold – but is only recognizable to those who are free of sin!

➕ 1D ✉ 13km (8 miles) southwest of Vathi ☎ (28220) 61261
🕐 7am–sunset 💷 Free 🍴 Two tavernas (€) on the Vathi road

PALAIOCHORA

Formerly a fishing village, and one-time haunt of hippies, Palaiochora now has universal appeal, with its fine setting below rugged mountains, its excellent beaches and relaxed atmosphere. It is not overwhelmed by tourism and sits on a small peninsula, crowned by the stone walls of a Venetian castle. Beneath it are two beautiful bays: to the east a sheltered but shingle and pebble beach, to the west a long stretch of wide golden sands shaded by tamarisk trees and very popular with windsurfers.

Venizelos, the main street, is lively at night, when the road is closed to traffic and taverna tables spill out onto the pavements. Despite its popularity the centre has not lost all its Cretan character – locals still frequent the cafés and fishermen land their catch at the quayside. Linked to coastal villages by a regular ferry service, the resort makes an excellent base for exploring southern Crete, and is well placed for hikers, with coastal and mountain

walks. There are also weekend boats to the tiny island of Gavdos (► 167).

🔁 3E ✉ 80km (50 miles) southwest of Chania 🍴 Tavernas and retaurants (€–€€) 🚌 Regular service to Chania ⛴ Ferries to Sougia, Agia Roumeli, Loutro, Hora Sfakion (Chora Sfakion) and Gavdos

ℹ (028230) 41507

RODOPOU PENINSULA

The remote and rugged Rodopou peninsula extends 18km
(11 miles) from the low-lying coast west of Chania. The roads only
go as far as the hamlet of Afrata and the main village of Rodopou.
Beyond this the peninsula is uninhabited, the access limited to
rough tracks and footpaths. There are good walks in the
mountainous interior, but the tracks can be rough and there is very
little shade. At the northeastern tip of the peninsula lie the scant
Graeco-Roman remains of the Sanctuary of the goddess Diktynna,
excavated by the Germans during World War II. Statues from the
temple, which were discovered here, are now in the Chania
Archaeological Museum (► 159). The easiest way to reach the
remains is to take a boat excursion from Chania
or Kolimbari. Part of the attraction is the pretty,
sheltered cove below the sanctuary, ideal for
swimming. Going by car entails a rough ride and
half an hour's walk. On the west coast, the
isolated little Church of Agios Ioannis is reached
by a rough, dusty track from Rodopou, taking two
to three hours. This is the route taken by
thousands of pilgrims every year on 28 and 29
August (St John the Baptist's Day) to witness the
baptism of boys with the name of John (Ioannis).

✚ 3B ✉ West of Chania Bay 🍴 Simple cafés and tavernas in Afrata and
Rodopou (€) 🚌 Limited service to the village of Rodopou

SOUDA BAY ALLIED WAR CEMETERY

Sheltered by the Akrotiri peninsula to the north, Souda Bay is
Crete's largest natural harbour. Laid out on a neatly tended lawn,
sloping down to the water, are the graves of 1,497 Allied soldiers
who died defending Crete in World War II. The names of the
soldiers, many of whom lie in unknown graves, are listed in the
Cemetery Register, which is kept in a box at the entrance to the
building. Of the total Allied force on the island of 32,000 men,

18,000 were evacuated, 12,000 were taken prisoner and 2,000 were killed.

➕ 5C ✉ 5km (3 miles) southeast of Chania harbour 🚌 Service from Chania to Souda Bay

SOUGIA

Set against the backdrop of the Samaria hills, this former fishing port is rapidly expanding into a tourist resort. Remotely located at the end of a long twisting road from Chania, it was first discovered by backpackers, but more and more tourists are coming for the long pebble beach, translucent blue waters, simple tavernas and coastal and mountain walks. Accommodation has improved greatly over the years. Just to the east of the Souganos River mouth, a few Roman relics survive from the ancient port, which served the Graeco-Roman city of Eliros, 5km (3 miles) to the north. To the west a fine Byzantine mosaic, now in the Chania Archaeological Museum (➤ 159), was discovered where the modern church stands. Three kilometres to the west of the village, reached by a local boat or on foot over the cliffs (70–90 minutes) lie the classical Greek and Roman ruins of the ancient city of Lissos.

➕ 3D ✉ 70km (43 miles) southwest of Chania 🍴 Simple tavernas in the resort (€) 🚌 Service from Chania

a drive around the Akrotiri Peninsula

Head east from Chania towards the airport. At the top of a long uphill section, at a broad junction, turn left and follow signs for the Venizelos Graves. In 2km (1.2 miles), by a supermarket, turn left and then left again. After 50m (55 yards) turn left to the parking area.

Stone slabs mark the graves of Eleftherios Venizelos (1864–1936), Crete's famous statesman and his son, Sophoklis. The site commands a magnificent view of Chania, mountains and the coast.

Return to the main road and turn left. Turn left again at a roundabout towards the airport, and follow signs for Agia Triada and Moni Gouvernetou. Make a final right turn, signed Moni Gouvernetou, and reach Moni Agia Triada.

The Venetian-influenced 17th-century monastery has a church with a fine Renaissance facade and a small museum.

On leaving the monastery, turn immediately right and drive through starkly beautiful hills and a ravine, to the Gouvernetou monastery (4.5km/2.8miles).

This isolated monastery dates from 1548 and has Venetian features. From the monastery a path, steep in its final sections (2.5 hours there and back), descends to a